101

DEFENSIVE AND CONDITIONING WATER POLO DRILLS

PETER J. CUTINO SR. and PETER J. CUTINO JR.

ISBN: 1-58518-315-6
Library of Congress Number: 00-108297

Book layout and cover design: Rebecca Gold
Drawings: Rosemarie Cutino Topper

Coaches Choice
P.O. Box 1828
Monterey, CA 93942
www.coacheschoice.com

For more information about the drills in this book and waterpolo in general visit our website at www.waterpolo.cutino.com.

This book is respectfully dedicated to the memory of
Coach Steve Heaston
(1946-1999)

ACKNOWLEDGMENTS

Over the years, special thanks are extended, to all of the players and coaches whom we have had the opportunity to work with, and compete against. The challenges created in water polo competition best describes the basis of what sports should be: To try to imbue a sense of honor, genuine team spirit, respect for opponents and to reflect the notable and noble sentiment of the human spirit in striving to attain a goal.

Peter J. Cutino Sr.
Peter J. Cutino Jr.

PREFACE

This book reflects a combined fifty years of coaching and thirty-five years of actual competition as players. Our experiences include every level of competition from age group and high school to collegiate and international competition. It is our intent to add to the information available for development of coach and player in the sport of water polo.

Peter J. Cutino Sr.
Peter J. Cutino Jr.

CONTENTS

25m or 30m	25- or 30-meter course length
⊗	Offensive player with the ball
◯	Offensive player
X	Defensive player
←———	Movement of the player
∧∧∧	Dribbler
– – – ◄ – – –	Movement of the ball (pass)
◄———	Shot

CHAPTER 1

CONDITIONING DRILLS

Introduction

Since the sport of water polo takes place entirely in the water, swimming skill, mobility and endurance are essential requirements. Effective swimming drills include everything from short, intense swims to longer, slower workouts. The effectiveness of each drill depends on factors such as the swimmer's level of skill, age, body development, practice time available, and even the season of the year. One advantage to conditioning for water polo is that most of the swimming can be done with a water polo ball.

For a water polo player, leg strength development is key. All motion — lateral, forward, backward, and vertical — depends on natural ability and leg strength. Players' leg strength determines how well they will be able to come up high in the water, and their ability to lunge. The full range of motion of the legs allows a player to use the eggbeater combined with the scissor kick for quick and effective lateral moves, hooks and turns.

When conditioning for water polo, all swimming strokes and variations should be practiced. Sculling movements, for example, help develop strength in the arms and wrists. Besides using different strokes, swimmer should include all types of distances and repeats in order to prepare for water polo. Fartlek training (continuously swimming while switching from a slow tempo to a fast one and so forth), is a vital exercise to use for conditioning. The more familiar swimmers are with the entire aquatic environment, the more adaptable they will be to the sport of water polo.

Water polo players without a swimming background not only limit their careers, but also make it more difficult to reach their full potential. With age comes maturity and wisdom in water polo, but solid aquatic mobility is necessary to enhance water polo skills.

The list of outstanding swimmers who also played water polo is long, and includes Biondi, Morales, Rocca, Bottom, Spitz and Nader. There have also been many great water polo players who were exceptional swimmers, including Schumacher, Thomas, Saari, Figueroa and many NCAA champions and All-American swimmers.

A relatively unknown swimmer, Chris Humbert, has been the leading scorer for the United States Olympic team in the last two Olympics. He has posted outstanding times in both the sprints and long distance swimming (20 seconds for the 50-yard freestyle, low 50 seconds for the 100-yard backstroke, and in the low 16 minutes for 1500 meters). Activity in both sports leads to success in both sports. In addition, weight training and circuit training are valuable conditioning supplements for every sport.

#1 STROKE VARIATIONS DRILL

Objective: To practice specific water polo swimming strokes designed for more resistance than normal swimming strokes.

Description: A water polo individual medley of the following strokes is an excellent warm-up for 200-, 400- or 800- meter distances. Butterfly, using a flutter kick and keeping the head up; backstroke, using an eggbeater kick; human stroke (dog paddle), using an eggbeater kick; and the crawl stroke, swimming with the head up, the back arched and the leg kick breaking the surface of the water.

Variation: Same drill using shorter arm strokes to be able to receive the ball quickly.

Coaching point:

- Distance swims of 1500 meters (or distances as determined by the ability of team members) should be used early in the season, with a time trial every other week. This is a good way to develop long term conditioning.

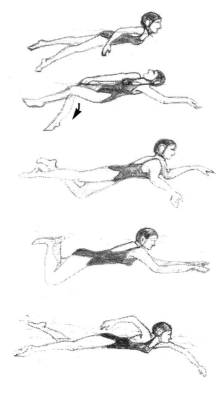

#2 100 STROKES DRILL

Objective: To improve overall conditioning.

Description: Players swim freestyle with their head up and must take 100 strokes in one length of the pool.

Variations: Build progressively, starting with 20 strokes, then 40, 60, 80 and finishing with 100 strokes.

Coaching Points:

- If a player is close to the end of the pool and has not reached 100 strokes, the player must take strokes in place until reaching 100.

- Player should stay semi-vertical and count out strokes.

- Quick armstrokes are used in key situations, (i.e., for passes, moving into position, getting free, etc.).

#3 CORNER POOL EGGBEATER TECHNIQUE DRILL

Objective: To practice proper eggbeater techniques.

Description: Players get on their backs in the corner of the pool. While holding on to each side of the pool, the players practice the proper eggbeater technique.

Variation: Although not as effective, the players can do the drill while on their stomachs.

Coaching Points:

- This teaching drill is effective for correcting leg actions.
- Some players rely too much on the scissors kick, which inhibits the ability to change directions quickly.

#4 SPIDER EGGBEATER DRILL

Objective: To help condition the players' legs while they maintain a horizontal position.

Description: Players begin in a straight line. On the first whistle, the players get their hips up. On the second whistle, they go from vertical to horizontal using the eggbeater kick. The kick is done close to the surface of the water while the hands use either the human stroke or breaststroke arm pull.

Variation: Distance can be extended to 25 meters or more.

Coaching Point:

- The more the players get into a horizontal position, the more they improve their ability to make quicker turns and moves. They can also cover more area and get up higher when going from horizontal to vertical while playing defense or during offensive opportunities.

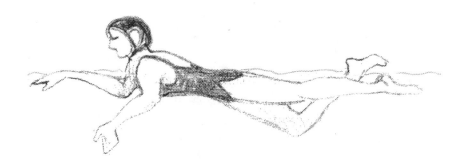

#5 PROUD BREASTSTROKE DRILL

Objective: To improve body balance and movement in the vertical position while maintaining a high position in the water.

Description: Players begin in a straight line. From the vertical position, players use short breaststroke arm pulls in order to stay upright while making quick, short breaststroke leg kicks. Keep head, shoulders and chest out of the water.

Variation: Use eggbeater kick instead of a breaststroke kick.

Coaching Points:

- Also called vertical breaststroke. Make sure the players stay high in the water without bobbing up and down.
- Strong strength drill.

#6 EGGBEATER STATIONARY LEG DRILL

Objective: To improve leg conditioning.

Description: Players begin in the center of the pool, in a random formation. Drill starts with players using their hands and feet to tread water. On the coach's whistle, all players react and copy the position of the coach's arms. The final position, with both arms up, should be a challenge and held for 60 seconds.

Variations: Some of the arm positions to use in this drill include: hands on top of the head, one arm straight up, both arms straight up, both arms straight up with hands together, grabbing elbows behind the head, and arms extended sideways. This drill can also be done with an adjustable weight belt around the players' waists to increase leg strength.

Coaching Points:

- Best to use this drill at the end of practice, for six to ten minutes.

- If used at the beginning of practice, the drill should be of short duration. Be sure of a good warm-up prior to the drill.

- This drill should only be done after the players are in good physical condition. Be aware of the potential for too much stress on the legs.

7 MIDGET EGGBEATER WITH ARM STROKE DRILL

Objective: To practice proper eggbeater technique while conditioning legs.

Description: Players begin in a straight line. Players should keep knees up while in the tuck position. Arm stroke can be a breaststroke or a human stroke.

Variation: Distance can be extended to 25 meters or more.

Coaching Points:

- Emphasize keeping the knees up when in the vertical position.

- When players in a vertical position allow the legs to stay extended, it prevents a quick change of direction or mobility.

#8 FEET FIRST, BELLY FLOAT, REVERSE BREASTSTROKE ARM PULL DRILL

Objective: To improve body balance and movement in the water from various body positions.

Description: Players begin in a straight line. Players swim on their stomachs, going backwards (feet first) using a reverse breaststroke arm pull while keeping their head up.

Variations: It may be necessary to use a slight flutter kick to keep the legs up. This drill can also be performed with the players swimming backwards while on their back, going feet first, while using a breaststroke arm pull. Another variation is a feet first, back float, breaststroke arm pull.

Coaching Point:

*   Although it is a fun drill, it emphasizes water adaptation.

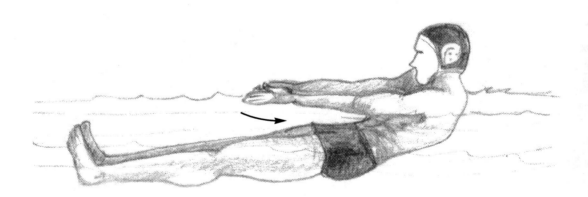

#9 FRONT TO BACK TO FRONT SPRINT DRILL

Objective: To improve player's ability to change strokes and positions while swimming.

Description: Players begin in a straight line across the pool. On the first whistle, players move to the two-meter line. On the second whistle, they sprint using a crawl stroke with their head up. On the next whistle, they roll and swim looking backwards, as if for a pass. On the following whistle, they roll back on their stomach and swim using a crawl stroke. Players continue rolling front to back to front until they reach the end of the pool.

Variation: Distance can be extended to 25 meters or more. Instead of full backstroke arm movements, the players can take half-strokes in order to adjust more quickly if a ball is passed to them.

Coaching Point:

- This is a motivating drill. When possible, the coach on the deck should walk with each line until the sprint is over.

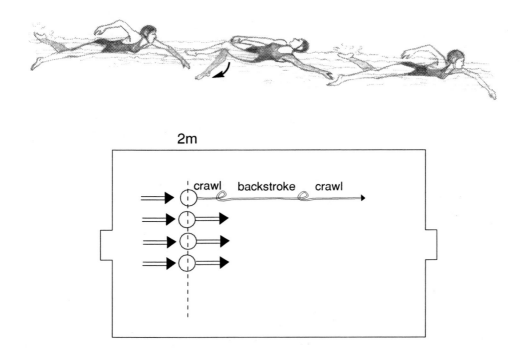

#10 CORKSCREW DRILL

Objective: To improve overall conditioning.

Description: Using only head-up freestyle strokes, each player must dive and roll in a zigzag pattern touching alternate lane lines with each change of direction.

Variation: Distance can be extended to 25 meters or more.

Coaching Point:

- Players should make as many turns as possible in one length.

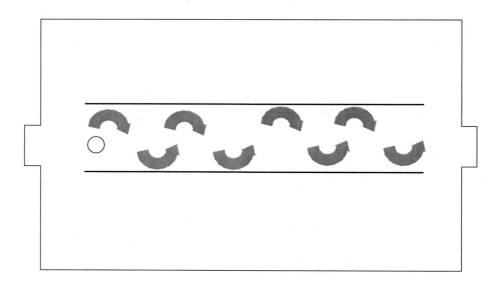

#11 JUMP AND SWIM DRILL

Objective: To improve overall conditioning.

Description: Players begin by swimming head-up freestyle and jump up when they hear the whistle. During the first set, the players raise their right hand as they jump. In the second set, they raise their left hand. During the third set, they raise their right and then their left hand. In the fourth and final set, they raise their right hand then their left hand and then both hands.

Variations: Coaches can add any number of different variations. For example, after each jump, the players must either wait for the whistle before they continue or continue swimming on their own. Players might jump laterally or forward at each whistle, or maintain a high eggbeater position after each jump.

Coaching Point:

- Jumps should be as high as possible. "Show your suit."

#12 CRAB WALK DRILL

Objective: To improve overall conditioning

Description: Players swim head-up freestyle for five strokes then start a reverse, high horizontal eggbeater until the whistle blows. Drill continues for four-to-eight lengths of the pool.

Variation: Players add a jump after the whistle blows, before swimming forward again.

Coaching Point:

- Vary the length of time for the reverse eggbeater. Tell the players the harder they work, the shorter the eggbeater time.

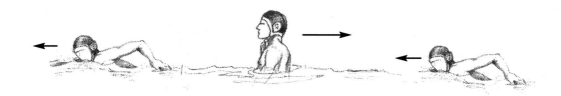

#13 ZIGZAG DRILL

Objective: To improve overall conditioning

Description: Four to six players, spaced two meters apart, form a line and begin doing the eggbeater with both hands up. The last player in the line swims head-up while zigzagging between the other players. When that player has reached the front of the line, the next player at the end of the line starts the same drill.

Variations: Player moves between the other players while encountering no resistance, medium resistance or heavy resistance. Drill can also include the moving player maneuvering through the other players with a ball, again, meeting no resistance, medium resistance or heavy resistance.

Coaching Points:

- During the variations using a ball, the other players cannot touch the ball, and should challenge the moving player without using their hands.

- The player swimming should keep the ball close at all times.

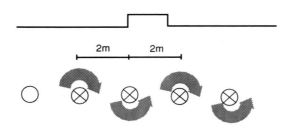

#14 BACKWARD TURN AND GO DRILL

Objective: To improve overall conditioning while emphasizing quick starts, turns and sprints.

Description: Players begin in a straight line across the pool. On the first whistle, players get hips up, facing away from the opposite end. On the second whistle, using the eggbeater kick and alternate hand motions (creating water action), they go backwards for approximately 10 meters. On the third whistle, players turn and sprint to the opposite end.

Variation: Distance can be extended to 25 meters or more.

Coaching Point:

• This is a motivating drill. When possible, the coach on the deck should walk with each line until they sprint.

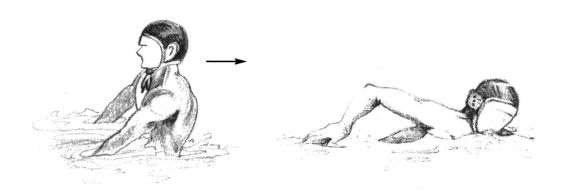

#15 LANE LINE TO LANE LINE DRILL

Objective: To improve body balance while emphasizing side to side movement and directional change.

Description: With the floating lane lines in the pool, players line up in one lane. On the whistle, they touch one lane line and then move sideways and touch the other lane line. Length of time for this drill can vary depending on the ability of the players.

Variation: A lane line is approximately nine feet wide. This drill can also be run using every other lane line, creating 18-foot distances.

Coaching Points:

- This can be a large group drill, with the intensity being controlled by the coach.

- This can be an effective low intensity drill.

#16 BALL ON HEAD EGGBEATER DRILL

Objective: To improve leg conditioning.

Description: Players place a ball on top of their head while doing the egg-beater. Both hands are positioned directly over the ball with fingertips meeting at the top.

Variation: This can be done as a stationary or moving drill, going forward, backward or sideways. The ball can also be held above the head.

Coaching Point:

- As the players get tired, they will slowly slip their hands to the sides of the ball. Encourage them to keep their hands on top of the ball.

#17 CHANGE OF DIRECTION DRILL

Objective: To improve defensive movement while emphasizing quick reactions and direction changes.

Description: Set up six players in a line, each four meters apart. The coach on the deck makes arm signals indicating four directions of movement: forward, back, left and right. The coach varies the order and timing to keep the players off balance, while randomly blowing the whistle to show that a whistle doesn't always indicate a change of direction (possession). Players must react to the coach's directions, not the whistle.

Variation: Perform five or six short, maximum intensity sets to improve quick reactions. Longer sets can serve as a conditioning drill.

Coaching Points:

- Point out the players who don't react quickly enough or lag behind the group.

- Tell the players that the harder they work, the shorter the sets will be.

- Divide the players up into two or three groups and praise the best group, to help motivate the other groups to work harder.

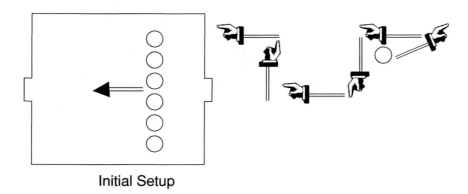

Initial Setup

#18 FOUR DIRECTION STOP AND GO SPRINT DRILL

Objective: To improve body balance and defensive movement while emphasizing quick reactions and direction changes.

Description: Players start in random positions in the center of the pool. Starting on the whistle, the players swim in the direction indicated by the coach until the next whistle and then change direction. When the coach points straight up, the players come up and stay as high in the water as possible. This intensity drill should not run more than 10 to 15 seconds at a time.

Variation: Perform the same drill, but with no whistle. The coach should just point or use a ball to indicate the direction he wants the players to swim.

Coaching Point:

- This drill works best with groups of four to six. Encourage competition between the groups to determine which is the most intense.

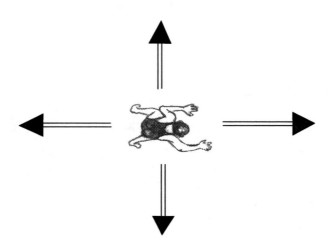

#19 BUDDY WEIGHT DRILL

Objective: To improve leg strength using the eggbeater kick against resistance.

Description: Players pair up, one behind the other. The players in back place their hands on the shoulders of the players in front. The players in front use eggbeater kicks and treading water arm motion to stay above the water. In five-second intervals: On the first whistle, the players in back press down on the front player's shoulders. On the second whistle, the rear players come up higher and put more weight on the front players. On the third whistle, the players in back straighten out their arms and put their full weight on the front players' shoulders, pushing them down in the water. After the players in back let go, the front players come as high out of the water as possible until the coach whistles the drill to stop. The two positions are then reversed.

Variation: The last whistle can be more than five seconds.

Coaching Point:

•   This is an excellent drill for the two-meter players.

#20 PARTNER LEAP FROG DRILL

Objective: To improve leg strength using the eggbeater against heavy resistance.

Description: Players pair up, one behind the other. This is a static drill where the players in back put their hands on their partner's shoulders, push down, and while using the resistance of the front players, spread their legs and "leap frog" over their partners, feet first. The players in front must not let their head go under water, while continuing the eggbeater. The two players are now in reverse positions, and continue to "leap frog" the length of the pool.

Variations: Distance can be extended up to 25 meters. Set up 25-meter races, disqualifying a team if any head goes under water.

Coaching Points:

- This is an excellent drill for two-meter players
- Advanced players should go over their teammates legs first, not head first.

#21 TRAILER HITCH DRILL

Objective: To improve arm strength using resistance.

Description: Players pair up. The front players use the crawl stroke while their partners hold on to the swimmers' ankles. The partners holding the ankles keep their arms extended. At the opposite end of the pool, partners change positions and swim back.

Variations: The players in back use a flutter kick and each twosome races against the other pairs. Dragged player can also be on his back.

Coaching Point:

- If more resistance is preferred, the players who are being dragged cross their legs and do not aid the swimmers.

2   1

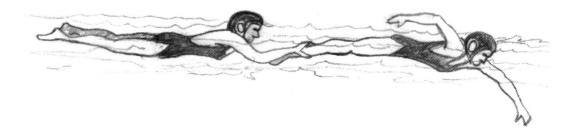

#22 WAR – EGGBEATER/FLUTTER KICK

Objective: To improve conditioning using resistance.

Description: Two players pair up. They begin by facing each other in a semi-vertical position with their hands on each other's shoulders and their arms extended. On the coach's whistle, they push against each other, using the eggbeater, until the coach declares a winner.

Variations: In the horizontal position, the kick used can be the flutter, breaststroke or eggbeater. Drill can also be performed with players beginning back-to-back, arms hooked together. On the whistle, they use the eggbeater kick to push against each other.

Coaching Points:

- Be sure these drill do not become excessive by allowing a player to completely back their opponent under water.

- This can be used as a competition where the winners go against other winners until there is a "champion." Players eliminated should stay in the water with their hands up.

#23 WAR — BACK-TO-BACK DRILL

Objective: To improve conditioning using resistance.

Description: Players play up and begin back-to-back, arms hooked together. On the whistle, they use the eggbeater kick to push against each other.

Variation: Drill can be performed with each player's hand on the other player's head, trying to sink each other. Same drill can be run using the other hand.

Coaching Point:

- Only do the hand on-the-head drill once or twice, as sore necks can result from extended competitions.

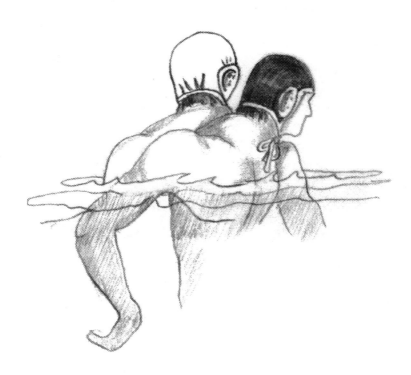

#24 THREE-WHISTLE CHANGE OF DIRECTION DRILL

Objective: To improve change of direction skills.

Description: Players begin lined up on the two-meter line. On the first whistle, they sprint until the second whistle, at which point they reverse and swim slowly back. A third whistle starts them sprinting forward again.

Variation: This drill can be a two-whistle drill with each whistle starting a sprint to the side of the pool.

Coaching Points:

- Emphasize keeping legs under the body and the head up when turning.

- Players should swim fast until they get back to the side of the pool.

- This is a fun drill that emphasizes water adaptation.

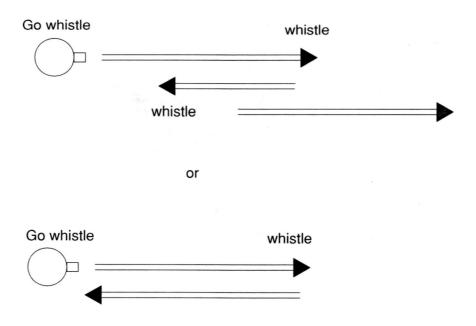

Two or three whistles in a 20-meter sprint

#25 COMPASS DRILL

Objective: To develop the ability to react to the ball, change directions and challenge an opponent who has possession of the ball.

Description: This drill requires five players, four forming a square and the fifth in the middle of the square. One of the perimeter players begins the drill by passing the ball to another perimeter player. The center player charges toward the player with the ball, who makes a shooting motion. The center player matches the perimeter player's hands (i.e., left to right and right to left). The ball is then passed to another perimeter player and the player in the center repeats the challenge.

Variations: The center player actually touches the player who has the ball, moving from player to player. A longer drill could include the center player trying to lunge block each perimeter player with the ball.

Coaching Point:

- The center position should be rotated through all five players every 10 to 15 seconds.

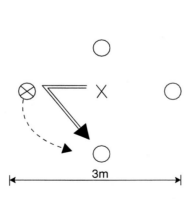

#26 ANIMAL CIRCUIT DRILL

Objective: To improve physical conditioning while building stamina and improving shooting skills.

Description: This drill is a continuous series of exercises. Players start at one end of the pool and swim the butterfly stroke with their head up to half-court. At half-court, they make three eggbeater jumps and then continue the eggbeater, with their hands behind their back, to the other end of the pool. Then they get out of the pool, walk behind the goal, jump back in again and swim the butterfly to half-court. This time at the halfway point, they face the cage, make a drive-in with a ball and shoot at the goal. After retrieving their shot, they swim head-up to half-court and make another drive-in and shot, this time at the other cage. The sequence can then be repeated.

Variations: The exercises in the circuit can be changed to include a rear-back (RB) from outside five meters instead of one of the drive-ins, or possibly three rear-backs at each end.

Coaching Points:

- Missed shots can be penalized with push-ups or squats during the time the players are out of the pool.

- Players should keep track of their shooting percentage.

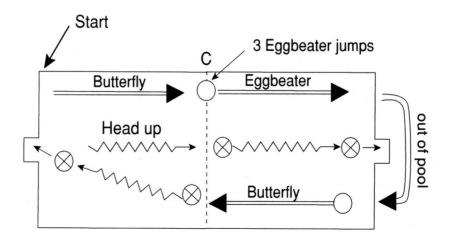

#27 QUICK START AND RETURN DRILL

Objective: To improve overall quickness in the water while emphasizing starts and turns.

Description: Players begin in a straight line near the side of the pool. On the coach's whistle, they sprint approximately three meters or until the whistle blows, then immediately sprint back to the side of the pool.

Variation: This drill can be run at opposite ends of the course at the same time.

Coaching Point:

- Emphasize keeping the legs under the body when turning and keeping the head up while sprinting back to the side of the pool.

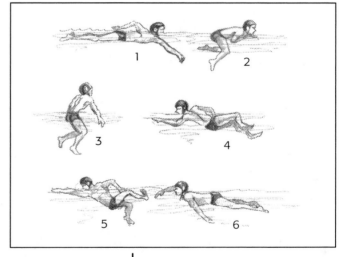

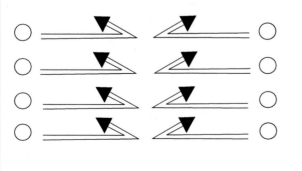

#28 STAIR STEP DRILL

Objective: To improve overall conditioning.

Description: The coach marks four to six distances, each farther away from the swimmers. On the whistle, the players swim head-up freestyle, full speed to the closest mark, then turn and swim back to the start. They continue swimming back and forth until the course is completed. Repeat the drill three times.

Variations: Run the same drill with the players dribbling a ball. They can also swim the stairs step distances out to the farthest distance and then back down to the shortest distance again.

Coaching Point:

• Players must make quick turns using the scissor kick.

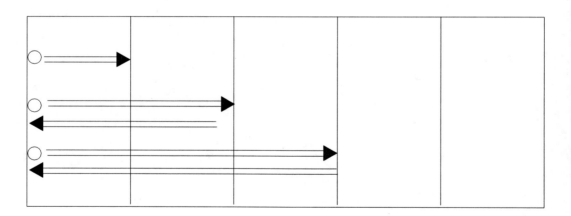

#29 CATCH AND PASS DRILL

Objective: To improve defensive positioning skills while increasing swimming speed.

Description: Players pair up with the player with the ball in the lead. The defensive players swim until they can establish an inside water position and hold off the offensive players with their back. Players then switch positions and repeat the drill in the opposite direction.

Variation: This can be either a continuous swimming drill, or a high intensity, short duration drill.

Coaching Point:

- Encourage swimmers to keep their head up and use quick, short arm strokes.

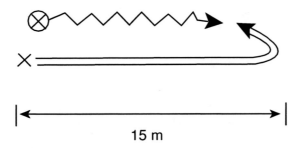

15 m

#30 FLOATING PULL-UPS DRILL

Objective: To improve shoulder and arm strength.

Description: Players line up along the side of the pool, placing two hands on top of the deck. On the first whistle, they raise themselves straight up as far as they can out of the water. On the second whistle, they lower themselves back down into the water.

Variation: A series of pull-ups can be used in between swimming sprints.

Coaching Points:

- At times, the coach should hold the players an extra long time in the up position.

- The coach should know the level and age of all players, and care should be taken with this drill to avoid injury.

#31 BOTTLES AND CHAIR DRILL

Objective: To improve leg conditioning using extra weight resistance.

Description: Players begin with a three-gallon jug with water in it (the amount depends on the player's ability and age level). Players are required to hold the jug over their head until all of the water drains out.

Variation: Folding chairs, weight belts, etc., can be used instead of a jug, with various time limits set for each item.

Coaching Points:

- There is a tendency to fill the water jug too full; always watch for potential injuries.

- This drill is not for young players.

- To avoid injuries, ensure that players have a good warm-up and stretching period before this drill.

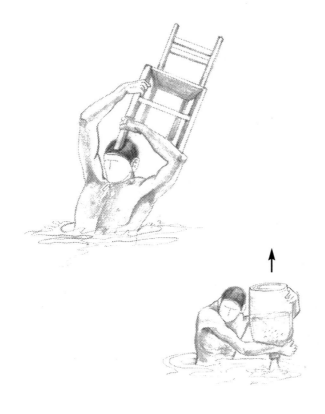

#32 LINE FORMATION BALL DRILL

Objective: To build teamwork, enhance communication between players and improve conditioning while practicing passing and receiving skills.

Description: Players are divided into two teams of six to ten players each and form two straight lines with players facing front to back. The first player in each line starts with a ball. On the coach's whistle, the ball is passed to the player immediately behind them. The ball continues backwards until reaching the last player in the line. That player immediately dribbles the ball to the front of the line and begins passing the ball down the line again. This is repeated until the players are in their original positions again. Each team must indicate they are done by an arm signal decided upon by the coach.

Variations: This drill can be done using all types of passes. Another variation has each team using more than one ball at a time.

Coaching Point:

- The coach can keep score and reward the winning team.

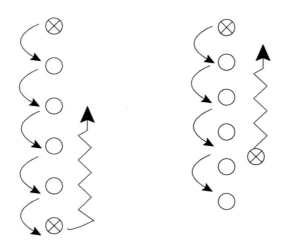

#33 RELAY DRILL

Objective: To increase teamwork and improve physical conditioning.

Description: This drill involves dividing the players into relay teams in such a way that the teams are as evenly matched as possible. Half of each team starts at one end of the pool and the other half starts at the other end. The coach determines which type of relay they will swim and which end will start first. On the whistle, the first players on each team begin the relay from opposite ends of the pool. When they reach the other end of the pool, the first players lined up on that end begin swimming back to the starting end. The relay continues until one team catches the other.

Variations: Any type of leg kick can be used, as well as any type of swimming stroke. Add a ball to make these dribbling relays.

Coaching Point:

- This drill is a great way to motivate players by having their teammates encourage them.

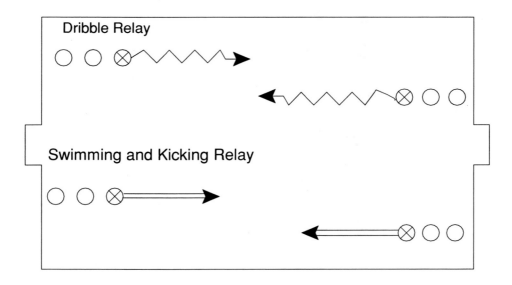

Dribble Relay

Swimming and Kicking Relay

#34 WILD HORSES DRILL

Objective: To improve leg strength using resistance.

Description: Players line up along the side of the pool with a belt around their chest or waist. Using surgical tubing to connect to the side of the pool or lane line, they pull against the resistance, while performing various kicks and strokes.

Variations: With the belt around their chest, players can use the eggbeater kick, first with their bodies facing away from the pool or lane line, and then facing the other direction. With the belt around their waist, players can use the backstroke (taking quick, half-strokes), the breaststroke (with full strokes), the flutter and eggbeater kicks (while holding a ball) and the crawl stroke (with their head up).

Coaching Point:

- The best way to enforce full resistance conditioning is to place large groups in a small area of the pool.

CHAPTER 2

INDIVIDUAL DEFENSIVE DRILLS

Introduction

Without a doubt, the most important phase of water polo is defense. It is vitally important that all field players be thoroughly trained in individual defensive skills and team defensive schemes. There is always room on a water polo team for a good defensive player. When a team has well-trained individual defenders it usually means that they will have a solid team defense as well.

All successful teams in the modern game of water polo have exceptionally strong individual and team defense. The individual defenders keep constant pressure on the offensive players. It is vital that they know the exact position of the ball at all times. Strong defensive play forces the offense to make mistakes in both their movement and their passing. Anticipation is the key to playing good "heads-up" water polo.

It is essential that defenders keep their eyes on the ball, anticipate where the ball will go, and be ready to counterattack when, or even before, the ball changes hands. For example, if the ball is in the air and it looks like the defensive team should gain control, an alert perimeter defender should initiate a fast break. Sometimes only a half of a body length advantage can lead to a score.

The following are defensive principles that become offensive principles:

- Anticipate. Take advantage of the right moment to tackle, to intercept, to swim, to pass and to shoot.

- Take the offensive two-meter player the length of the course.

- Keeping your hips up makes it easier to defend against the driver.

- Use your body position to force drivers to go the way you want them to go.

- On a free throw, protect against the back door.

- Protect the middle; watch for short passes; stay high with your hands at the surface and be ready to move.

- Keep your hips high when defending two-meter players; always try to keep them off balance.

- Keep offensive players away from the scoring area
- Fewer splashes leads to fewer fouls
- Constantly keep offensive players off balance and never allow them to rest.
- Man-to-man defense does not mean you put your hand on the offensive player's shoulder, since this tells him where the defensive player is and makes it easier for him to pass the ball.
- Challenge all passes
- Be aware of the 35-second clock, anticipation is the key.
- "Steal the ball" is a golden rule.

#35 THE LUNGE BLOCK DRILL

Objective: To practice defensive techniques that inhibit the ability of offensive players to pass, and impede them from regaining their balance and further assisting the offense.

Description: This technique is used on the perimeter and in the backcourt. The defensive player must be aware of the position of the passer's hips. As the passer turns and rolls to pass, the defender uses leg kick to get up onto the offensive player, by putting one hand on the passer's chest while the other hand matches the offensive player's hand that has the ball. The move should sink the offensive players by pushing them away and down into the water.

Variation: The offensive players can practice their pass and drive technique on the defensive players.

Coaching Points:

- Emphasize that the defensive players must be aware of the position of the hips of the offensive players before they roll to pass, in order to anticipate and block the pass.

- All passes, when feasible, should be challenged.

- Care should be taken to protect the offensive player from grabbing and countering.

#36 GRAB BLOCK DRILL

Objective: To practice defensive techniques that inhibit the ability of offensive players to pass, and impede them from regaining their balance and further assisting the offense.

Description: This drill technique is best used against the side of the pool or against the perimeter of the field of play, and when the offensive players are in a vertical position, close to their own two-meter player. As the offensive players attempt to pass, the defenders reach around their waist, pulling the offensive player towards the defender, sinking them slightly, while the defender's other arm and hand is raised to match the passer's hand.

Variation: Defender can attempt to steal the ball by reaching underneath.

Coaching Point:

- This is an aggressive pull since the offensive player is in the act of passing.

#37 DIRECT THE DRIVER DRILL

Objective: To improve individual defensive skills against drivers.

Description: This drill involves two-meter players, offensive drivers with a ball and defenders. The defensive players establish position on the drivers, allowing a driving lane away from the triangle in front of the cage. If the drivers attempt to drive to the other side, the defensive players must hold their position (and possibly force an offensive foul). When the offensive players initiate the drive, they should be pushed away from the center and toward the side.

Variations: This drill can be run with the offense attacking at "walk-through" speed (50%) or at game speed (100%).

Coaching Points:

- Defensive players must have correct body position. They should react immediately and try to take two strokes for every stroke the offensive player takes.

- When the offensive players reach the four-meter line, they should look for a pass from the two-meter player, while the defensive players should look to block the pass.

#38 CATCH AND DRIVE-OFF FOR POSITION DRILL

Objective: To improve a defender's ability to synchronize strokes with an opponent who has a lead, in order to force the offensive player to hook-out or stop.

Description: Players pair up and the offensive players begin a 15 to 20 meter drive with a half-body lead. While catching up, the defenders attempt to get their swim stroke in cadence between the drivers' strokes. The defenders don't stop until their body is between the offensive player and the goal.

Variations: This drill can be run with the offense attacking at "walk-through" speed (50%) or at game speed (100%).

Coaching Point:

- Coaches should be positioned so they can referee and determine when fouls occur.

#39 HALF COURT DRIVER DEFENSE DRILL

Objective: To improve defensive positioning skills by learning to stay with offensive drivers and altering their intended course.

Description: Offensive players and defensive players line up at half court. The offensive players start toward the goal and the defensive players work to position themselves slightly to one side of the drivers to prevent them from going where they want to go.

Variation: The distance can be extended to 25 meters.

Coaching Points:

- Exactly how far to the side the defensive players position themselves is determined by each player's speed and ability. If the players are close to being equal in ability, the player going forward (offense) has the advantage over the player going backwards.

- This drill illustrates the first fundamental of a pressing man-to-man defense.

- Emphasize that the defenders should not position themselves too close to the offensive players.

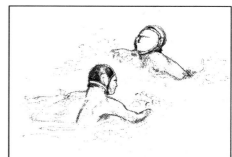

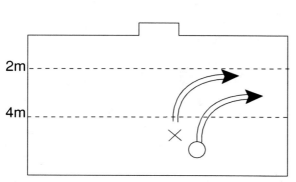

#40 PROTECTING CENTER COURT DRILL

Objective: To inhibit a driver from penetrating in the triangle of the defense.

Description: This drill involves two-meter players (who are passers only), drivers (who only go for inside water) and defenders. The defenders, with their hips pointing toward the goalie, attempt to keep the drivers away from center cage by playing the drivers off their shoulder and staying to the inside of center pool. When the offensive players attempt to drive past the defenders, the defenders aid the drivers' movement by pushing against their side as they stroke, thus helping to "turn them out."

Variations: This drill can be run with the offense attacking at "walk-through" speed (50%) or at game speed (100%).

Coaching Points:

- Too often the defenders are too close to the offensive players.

- If the drivers are too strong to be diverted, the defenders must use the offensive players' momentum to help make them wing-out early.

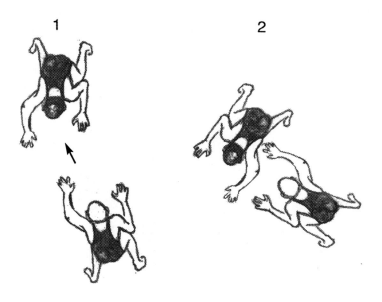

#41 FULL COURT, PLAYER-ON-PLAYER POSITION DRILL

Objective: To improve defensive positioning skills against counterattacks and drives.

Description: Players pair up and begin the drill with the offensive players taking five to seven strokes and then stopping. The defensive players, swimming with them, must cut them off while pushing them away from the center of the field. When the offensive players stop, the defensive players take two or three more strokes and then come around into the correct defensive position (lined up on the offensive player's shoulder). The defensive players give a signal once they get into position. Then the offensive players continue, and the drill is repeated. Players change positions every lap.

Variation: The offense players increase intensity and try to get inside water.

Coaching Points:

- This is one of the most important defensive drills.

- Defensive players should always be in a horizontal position; their hips should not drop as they come around into position.

- Both players must keep their head up.

- Emphasize that the defensive players must stay between the offensive players and the cage at all times.

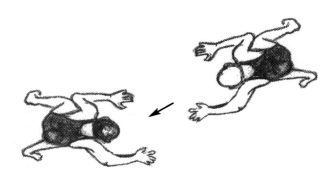

#42 ONE-ON-ONE DRIVE DRILL

Objective: To inhibit a driver from penetrating into the triangle of the defense.

Description: This drill involves two-meter players (who are passers only), drivers (who start at six to eight meters and only go for inside water) and defenders. The defenders attempt to keep the drivers away from center cage by playing the drivers off their shoulder, with their hips pointing toward the goalie.

Variation: The same drill can be run with the drivers starting from either side or the center of the field.

Coaching Points:

- The coach needs to control this drill because it can get too aggressive.

- Try to keep players from penetrating the triangle area shown in the diagrams.

Starts at six - eight yards   From Center   From Right Side

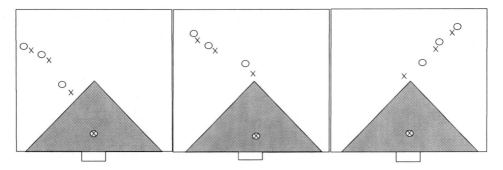

Defenders' Positions on Drivers

#43 BETWEEN KICKS, BALL STEAL DRILL

Objective: To improve defensive skills while emphasizing stealing the ball.

Description: Players pair up with the defensive players positioned behind the offensive players. The defensive players use their legs to move forward and, without splashing, lean into the offensive players and steal the ball. The defenders must time their move so it takes place between the time the offensive players stop and begin moving again.

Variation: This drill should be performed using both left and right arms.

Coaching Points:

- This is primarily a perimeter defensive move.

- This move can also be used to sink the ball by putting the defender's hand on top of the ball.

- This technique can also be used by the two-meter guard on the two-meter offensive player .

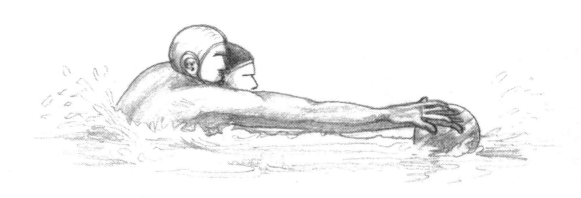

#44 REACH UNDER AND FLIP DRILL

Objective: To improve defensive skills while emphasizing stealing the ball.

Description: Players pair up with the defensive players positioned behind the offensive players. The defensive players act as if they are moving to one side of the offensive players, in order to get them to turn slightly away. The defensive players then quickly slide to the opposite side and reach under the water and flip the ball over the offensive players' arm, shoulder or head. The defenders then roll over, placing the offensive players behind them as they dribble away or pass.

Variation: This drill can be used against the side of the field of play or on the perimeter.

Coaching Point:

- Emphasize the importance of making the offensive players turn away by making a good fake move.

#45 LOOSE BALL DRILL

Objective: To improve the defender's ability to aggressively challenge for the ball.

Description: From the deck, a ball is thrown in between an offensive and defensive player, who both attempt to recover the ball and quickly toss it to a safe area. At the same time, the other two offensive and defensive players also try to challenge for control of the ball.

Variation: The ball can be thrown in the air or off the water between the opposing players.

Coaching Point:

- The coach can pre-determine who gets the ball while looking for quickness and aggressiveness.

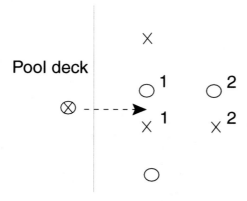

#46 TURN HAND UP DRILL

Objective: To inhibit the offensive player's opportunities to receive the ball.

Description: Drill begins with a defensive player between two offensive passers, approximately seven meters apart. When the first offensive player picks up the ball, the defender takes two strokes towards the other player, rolls on his back and lifts his hand toward the ball being passed. After the second offensive player receives the ball, he holds it until the defender swims back to his original position, then the drill repeats in the opposite direction. Players rotate positions after every twelve passes.

Variation: The same drill can be run with two defenders between three offensive players.

Coaching Point:

- The defender must challenge every pass, putting his hand up in the direction of the flight of the ball. This move may lead to an interception of a bad pass, or a deflection that a teammate can recover.

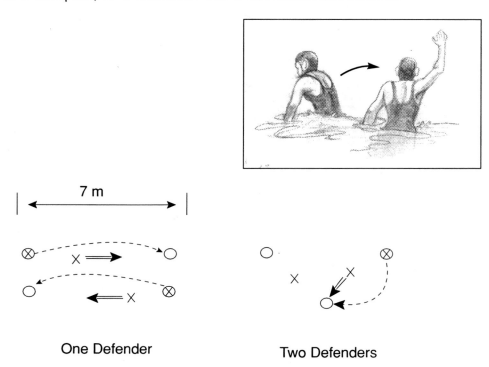

7 m

One Defender   Two Defenders

CHAPTER 3

THE TWO-METER
DEFENDER DRILLS

Introduction

Effective scouting is the foundation for a good two-meter defense. An under-standing of the abilities and tendencies of the opposing two-meter player is invaluable in determining how to correctly guard that player. The primary goal for all defensive teams should be to prohibit the ball from being passed to the offensive two-meter player. With few exceptions, the two-meter guard should be one of the two best players on any team (with National and Olympic teams this may not always be the case because of the special abilities of all-star play-ers).

Some important principles to keep in mind when instructing two-meter defensive players include defensive positioning and physical skills. In actual competition, the best way to defend a two-meter player is usually in front of, or to the side of the player. Which position to use is determined by the type of perimeter pressure being applied by teammates, or the drop-back system the defense is using at the time.

As a general rule, the following defensive principles apply to defending the two-meter player:

- If the defender is behind the two-meter player, he should guard to the turning or shooting side (also known as the power side) of the offensive player.

- The following guidelines can be used for defending a two-meter player except when using a specific guarding technique on a specific player:

    - If the ball is in the backcourt, front the offensive player.

    - If the ball is half way down the court, take a position on ball side.

    - If the ball is in the frontcourt, within the length of the goal, the defender's head should be ball side.

- If the two-meter player is outside the goal posts, the position of the defender's body is ball side (with proper pressure). If the two-meter player is more than one meter outside the post of the goal, then the defender must get between the two-meter player and goal. Eliminate all goals from two meters. Pick-up the two-meter player as soonas possible and continue to defend him all of the time. Take the physical part of the game to the limit. Communicate constantly with the goalie. Stair step to cover the two-meter area.

- In addition to proper positioning, a two-meter defender should have the ability to quickly and effectively counterattack. Swimming speed and endurance are necessary attributes. Leg strength cannot be over-emphasized. A two-meter defender should have the ability to use proper leg techniques to keep the two-meter player off balance and maintain constant pressure during a game.

#47 TWO-METER DEFENSIVE POSITION DRILL

Objective: To improve two-meter defensive skills by practicing proper positioning in order to inhibit a two-meter player's ability to receive the ball.

Description: This is a series of drills in which passes are made to the two-meter player from different areas of the field. The defenders must adjust their position depending on the location of the ball. The foundation of defense is ball side. When the ball is in the backcourt, the defenders front the two-meter players. When the ball is in the frontcourt and the two-meter players are outside the goal posts, the defenders' position is between the two-meter players and the goal. When the two-meter players are between the goal posts, the defenders are on the ball side. When in doubt, the defenders should play to the power side (i.e., if the two-meter player is right handed, the defender plays on the left).

Variations: This drill can be run with the offense attacking at "walk-through" speed (50%) or at game speed (100%).

Coaching Points:

- The coach should insist that the defenders be ball side.

- Instruction should include when to move to the various positions. For example, if in a pressure defense then the two-meter defenders can move more easily into proper position. On a free throw or uninterrupted pass, however, they must be more conservative in their movement.

- The defender's head should always be on the ball side of the two-meter player's head (except when playing the two-meter player to the power side).

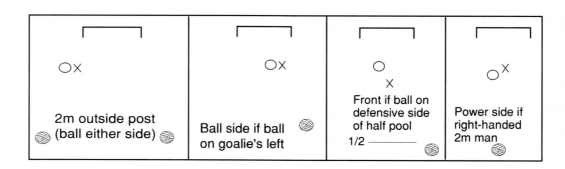

#48 BALL SIDE DRILL

Objective: To improve movement to the ball side of the two-meter players in order to inhibit passes to them.

Description: Drill begins with two offensive players on the seven-meter line making passes to each other. The two-meter defender is behind the two-meter player, and moves to the side that the ball is on by swimming around to the ball side. After the defender has assumed that position, the outside players pass the ball to the other side, and the two-meter defender moves to that side.

Variation: When the ball is inside of half-court, the two-meter defender slides ball side. When the ball is outside of half-court, the two-meter defender fronts the two-meter player.

Coaching Points:

- Passers should not pass the ball until the defender is on the ball side.

- The two-meter defenders must be aware that they only move if there is a good man-to-man defense or a situation that allows them to move ball side, such as the ball going out of bounds, while not committing a dead time ejection foul.

- The two-meter defenders do not move if there is a free or easy pass.

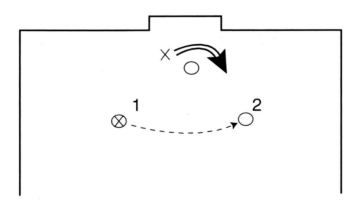

#49 TWO-METER CONSTANT CONTACT DRILL

Objective: To improve individual skills against the two-meter player.

Description: Players pair up, with the offensive players beginning on the two-meter line. The defensive players establish and maintain correct position (45-degrees behind) and show one arm in front to inhibit passes to the two-meter player. When the coach indicates a change in the position of the ball, the defenders must swim behind the two-meter players, without losing physical contact. The defenders must maintain their horizontal position until they reach the correct defensive position on the other side.

Variation: The offensive players increase their intensity and try to maintain position while the defensive players must make their way to the other side without committing an ejection foul.

Coaching Points:

- As the defensive players come around the offensive players, they should take several strokes, using the offensive players to help them move by pushing and pulling on them between strokes. This contact keeps the two-meter players off balance, which can sometimes cause them to become more preoccupied with the "struggle" than the game situation.

- Pressure is determined by whether it is a closely or loosely officiated game.

#50 BALL RETURN DRILL

Objective: To improve defensive skills including anticipation, reaction and ball handling.

Description: This drill simulates game situations where two players go for a loose ball. It is also a good drill for the two-meter defenders when they must get to a deflected or errant pass. The drill begins with two players about two meters apart. The first player makes wet passes near the second player, who must react and return the ball dry, as fast as possible. The return passes should be from the water, and be quick, firm and direct to the passer's hand. The wet passes can be to either side, in front of, or lobbed over the receiving player. Initial passes should vary so that the receiver cannot easily anticipate the next pass location. Switch positions after three to five series of 10 consecutive passes.

Variations: Drill can be expanded to three players, utilizing two passers (the ball can be returned to either of the two passers), or one passer (two receivers work to gain control of the loose ball).

Coaching Point:

- This is an excellent conditioning drill.

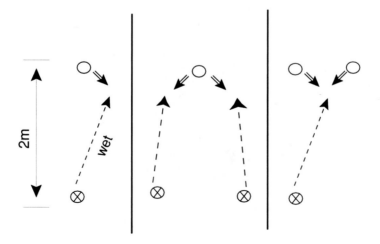

#51 HAND-IN-THE-BACK DRILL

Objective: To improve two-meter defensive skills by keeping two-meter players from shooting.

Description: Two players pair up with the defensive player positioned behind the offensive player. The defenders place their hand between the shoulder blades of the two-meter players, causing them to arch their back. It is very difficult to accurately shoot from that position.

Coaching Points:

- Caution must be used since this will be called a foul by some referees.

- This technique is used when the defensive player is out of position. It is to be used as a last resort, instead of taking an ejection.

#52 PUSH OPPOSITE AND REACH DRILL

Objective: To improve defensive skills while emphasizing proper positioning and stealing the ball

Description: Two pairs of players pass to each other, with the two defenders attempting to steal the ball. With the defender's head on the left of the offensive player's head, the defender uses his left hand to gradually push the offensive player's hip to the right, allowing the defender to slide his right hand and arm into a position to steal a pass.

Variation: Defensive players should practice this move from both sides.

Coaching Point:

- If this move is done too aggressively, it becomes a dangerous ejection foul at two meters.

#53 REACH UNDER AND SPLASH DRILL

Objective: To improve defensive skills by keeping the offensive player with the ball off balance and moving away from the goal.

Description: Players pair up with the defensive players positioned between the offensive players and the cage. Playing behind the offensive players, the defenders keep one arm extended between and under the offensive players' arms. Every time the offensive players reach for the ball, the defensive players move their hand and arm at the same time, and splash at the ball, so it moves away. This forces the offensive players to move away from the goal and reset in order to reach the ball.

Variation: This drill should be used against the side of the field of play or on the perimeter.

Coaching Points:

- This is a good technique when a no foul defense is desired.
- This is also a good technique for wing defense.

#54 JUMP STEAL DRILL

Objective: To improve defensive skills while emphasizing stealing the ball.

Description: Players pair up with the defensive player beginning about a half-meter from the offensive player. The defensive player uses a big kick (scissors or breaststroke), and jumps over the back of the offensive player, knocking the ball away.

Variation: This drill can be used against the side of the field of play or on the perimeter.

Coaching Points:

- Emphasize that the defenders must bring their legs up and "jump" with the kick, showing their opposite hand up.

- Defenders must clear the back of the offense players or this move will result in a foul being called.

CHAPTER 4

DEFENSE AGAINST THE COUNTERATTACK DRILLS

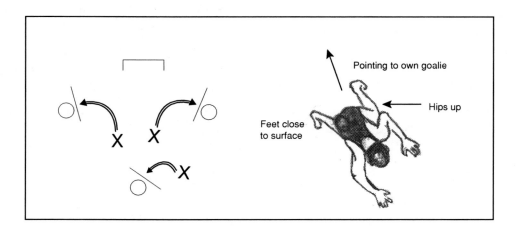

Introduction

Defense positions must always be anticipated when the team is on offense. The players who are the most talented on defense, and who do well in the overall game, are those who understand the situations that occur in the transition between defense and offense and offense and defense. They know the percentages and can anticipate the flow. This concept must be learned and understood in order to have an effective defense. Most goals against a novice team, for example, are scored off a miscue when their team has the ball on offense.

To defend against a counterattack, the following principles and concepts apply: The offensive front court system must be designed so that there are always a minimum of three players back, fairly close together at point, in order to direct and force counterattack players from driving down the center of the pool. Sometime during an attack, four players are committed to offense, but balance should be restored as quickly as possible. Know where the ball is at all times, do everything possible not to lose sight of the ball. Taking your eyes off the ball for more than a few seconds is too long.

Be ready to press the first pass to a field player, unless there is a more dangerous player closer to your goal. When possible, press the right side. Since most players are right handed, there is a natural tendency to protect the ball with the left hand, as they begin to handle the ball with the right hand. It is easier for a right-hander to catch a ball coming from the right in the scoring area and it is easier to advance the ball down the right side. On a pass from the left, the right-handed player must catch the ball across their face and body – which in most circumstances, causes the player to reduce his speed in order to handle the ball.

Learn to slow down an attack by using the following techniques:

- Stunt or feint so the offensive attackers are not sure which of their players will be defended. This can buy time while other team members are catching up to the counterattackers.

- Bait passes by making the counterattacker feel he is not being pressed, then surprise him by pressing.

- Force the counterattacker who has the ball to turn away from the offensive end of the pool.

- Attack the player with the ball suddenly and quickly.

- Occupy the passing lanes to force overhead passing, which is more difficult for a counterattacker to accurately accomplish. Overhead passes are also harder to see and catch.

- The more decisions counterattackers must make, the better the chances of them making mistakes. The foul and drop becomes a critical part of the defense, and players must learn the technique without committing an ejection foul.

- Look to intercept or inhibit all good passes.

- Understand that a team is most vulnerable when attacking, and realize the necessity to "jam back" on defense in order to cover and fill-in the area in front of the goal (the 2m - 6m area).

- Force the ball to the outside of the field of play. Protect the center of the field by positioning yourself so that counterattackers are forced away from the center.

- If a player is free, defend him so that he has the worst possible shooting angle. Be ready to return to guarding the player you have dropped off of, once the most dangerous player is covered.

- Be aware of communications from the goalie to help determine which offensive player to guard.

- Be aware of the shot clock.

- Learn all of the defensive formations.

#55 TWO-ON-ONE DEFENSE DRILL

Objective: To improve individual and team defensive skills during a two-on-one situation.

Description: This drill uses two offensive and two defensive players. The offense starts well behind half-court with a two-on-one advantage. The single defensive player must stunt back and forth to delay the offensive players until the trailer has time to catch up. The trailing defender must wait until the coach whistles before following the play.

Variations: The drill can be run at "walk through" speed (50%) both with and without a trailer. It can also be practiced at full speed to simulate a game situation.

Coaching Points:

- The single defensive players must not end up in the middle defending nobody. They must decide by the five-meter line which player they should cover. The following are general rules covering whom they should guard:

- The player closest to the cage.

- The player with the best angle.

- The player the goalkeeper directs them to take.

- Communication between the stunting defender and the trailer is very important. The stunting player should tell the trailer whom to cover.

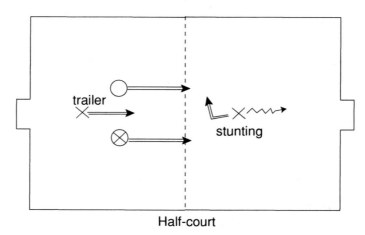

Half-court

#56 THREE-ON-TWO DEFENSE DRILL

Objective: To improve individual and team defensive skills during a three-on-two situation.

Description: This drill uses three offensive and three defensive players. The offense starts well behind half-court with a three-on-two advantage. The two defensive players must stunt back and forth to delay the offensive players until the trailer has time to catch up. The trailing defender must wait until the coach whistles before following the play

Variations: The drill can be run at "walk through" speed (50%) both with and without a trailer. It can also be practiced at full speed to simulate a game situation.

Coaching Points:

- Defensive players must stay with their offensive players. They should never leave the player closest to their cage.

- The stunting players should point to and tell the trailer whom to cover.

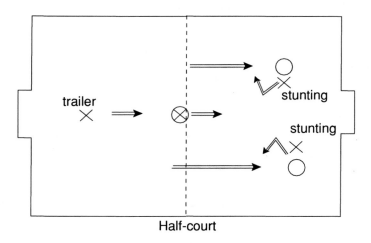

Half-court

#57 FOUR-ON-THREE DEFENSE DRILL

Objective: To improve individual and team defensive skills during a four-on-three situation.

Description: This drill uses four offensive and four defensive players. The offense starts well behind half-court with a four-on-three advantage. The three defensive players must stunt back and forth to delay the offensive players until the trailer has time to catch up. The trailing defender must wait until the coach whistles before following the play.

Variations: The drill can be run at "walk through" speed (50%) both with and without a trailer. It can also be practiced at full speed to simulate a game situation.

Coaching Points:

- The three defensive players must stay with their offensive players. They should never leave the player closest to their cage.

- Defenders must decide by the five-meter line which players they will cover.

- Communication between the stunting players and the trailer is very important. The stunting players should point to and tell the trailer whom to cover.

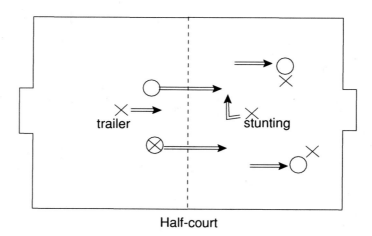

Half-court

#58 FIVE-ON-FOUR DEFENSE DRILL

Objective: To improve individual and team defensive skills during a five-on-four situation.

Description: This drill uses five offensive and five defensive players. The offense starts well behind half-court with a five-on-four advantage. The four defensive players must stunt back and forth to delay the offensive players until the trailer has time to catch up. The trailing defender must wait until the coach whistles before following the play.

Variations: The drill can be run at "walk through" speed (50%) both with and without a trailer. It can also be practiced at full speed to simulate a game situation.

Coaching Points:

- The three defensive players closest to the goal must stay with their offensive players. They should never leave the player closest to their cage.

- Defenders must decide by the five-meter line which players they will cover.

- Communication between the stunting players and the trailer is very important. The stunting players should point to and tell the trailer whom to cover.

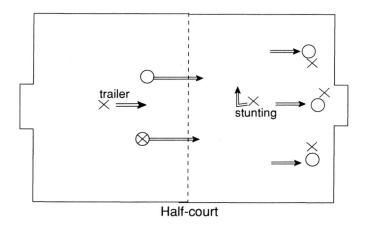

Half-court

81

#59 FIVE-ON-SIX DEFENSE OF A COUNTERATTACK

Objective: To improve team defense by practicing proper defensive positioning against a counterattack.

Description: The five defenders drop into a defensive formation that ensures that the back line is defended first. The outside defenders must pinch in so no shot is taken from point. This formation allows the player who was beaten to fill in on the top line. Against a 4-2 formation, a fourth defender must go to the back line if the offensive player in position six has the ball.

Variation: Practice defending both basic six-on-five counters – the 3-3 and the 4-2.

Coaching Points:

- If there is an opportunity, try to force the counterattack pass to the defending goalie's right side. That provides the best chance to slow down the counterattack, especially if there is no deep wing on the goalie's left. Since most players are right-handed, this makes them have to take the initial pass cross-face.

- The trailing defender must wait until the coach whistles before following the play.

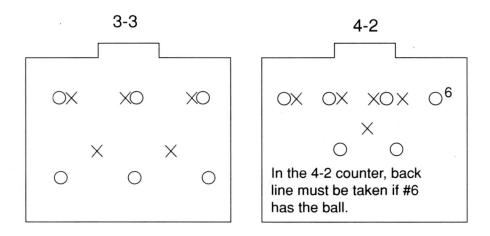

82

#60 CENTER PROTECTION DRILL

Objective: To improve team defensive skills when transitioning from offense to defense.

Description: Drill begins with players lined up in a 3-3 offense and the proper defense.

On the whistle, the ball is shot and the defenders must counterattack. The offensive players now take the proper defensive positions between the player they are guarding and the goal. They should have their feet close to the surface, their hips up and their buttocks pointing toward their own goalie. By properly positioning themselves, they try to force the counterattacking players toward the sides of the field of play.

Variations: This drill can be run with the offense attacking at "walk-through" speed (50%) or at game speed (100%).

Coaching Points:

- Emphasize that an offensive player should never be allowed to drive down the center of the field of play.

- Starting in the backcourt and wherever else they can, the defenders must position themselves to force the counterattacking players towards the sides of the field. This particularly applies to the two-meter defender.

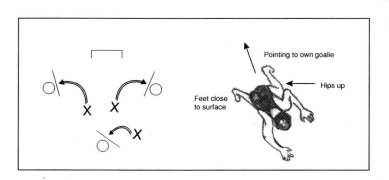

CHAPTER 5

TEAM DEFENSIVE DRILLS

Introduction

A simple definition for team defense is: To know what to expect from each other. Since team defense is easier to learn than team offense, it should be taught first. Available personnel skill levels and experience are major factors in determining what type of defense a coach chooses to run. For example, an extremely slow team will not be able to use a full court, tight man-to-man defense. They would be vulnerable to fast breaks from the backcourt. With a slow team, a coach may choose to play a loose man-to-man and pick up tight in the offensive end. Or they might use a zone or a drop back. (At times, even in a pressure man-to-man defense, there are situations that call for a drop back.)

Regardless of which defensive system is used, the ability to get into proper position is essential. Individual defensive players must be able to guard their opponents, and still be able to help defend other opponents in the surrounding area. When players help each other, and are aware of the limitations of space in the field of play, the defense becomes more successful. A good defense starts when a team is on offense and then continues as players in transition get back between the offensive players and the defensive goal.

Once position is set between an opponent and the goal, the defenders can move into positions that call for ball-side, in the lanes, or fronting their opponent defense.

The following principles apply to team defense:

- All defensive players should think as one. The ability to work as one unit is a key to playing successful defense.

- A strong offense is often generated by an effective defense. Players should attempt to anticipate and take advantage of all situations.

- A good perimeter defense should be able to protect the two-meter guard.

- Don't commit any unnecessary fouls. Even if an offensive player has inside water position with the ball, try to stop the shot without fouling. Be aware of the four-meter line. If you absolutely must foul, do so before the offensive player is inside the four-meter line. An ejection is less severe than a penalty throw.

- Give the driver a way to go, then anticipate and cut him off.

- When perimeter defenders are applying good, non-fouling pressure on the outside, the two-meter guard should play in front of the two-meter player (unless the ball is deep in the offensive court).

- If a defensive player commits a foul on the perimeter, he must look back to cover and intimidate a pass.

- Whenever possible, stop the wings from receiving the ball by pressing. Prevent a good pass from the wings by using a lunge block.

- In a triangle defense, prevent the offensive player from driving down the center of field of play. Crash back to where the ball is passed into the two-meter player position.

- Delay the ball from going into the two-meter area for as long as possible.

- Eliminate ejections on the perimeter. Play "smart water polo."

- Know your teammates abilities and tendencies; communication is the key.

- All players must be trained to initially break toward their offensive end the instant the ball changes hands.

- Constant pressure causes opponents to hurry, and that leads to mistakes. These mistakes can lead to poor passes, which set up the counterattack. The ability to anticipate those mistakes, and react quickly, can provide a successful counterattack.

- The counterattack is a great defensive team skill; it forces the other team to always back up. Counterattacks start when the other team has the ball.

- It is better to concentrate on defense the day before an important game.

- Always start a game in an aggressive manner.

#61 TWO-METER LINE DRIVER DEFENSE

Objective: To improve two-meter defensive skills by learning to use the two-meter line to help with defense and practice turning and facing the passer.

Description: The defenders cover the drivers as they go to the two-meter line. When the drivers hook, as if to receive the ball, the defensive players turn toward the two-meter players who have the ball. They should stay in the passing lane, so that if a pass is made to their man, it must go over the defenders' head. The defenders then roll to guard the drivers closer once they have the ball. If the drivers go to the two-meter defenders' right, the defenders turn left towards the passer. If the drivers go to the two-meter defenders' left, the defenders turn right towards the passer. This technique can also be used each time a driver stops as if to receive the ball.

Variation: Drill should be practiced with the drivers taking both left and right routes against the defenders.

Coaching Point:

- Start practicing this drill very slowly while the players learn and under stand these defensive principles. It takes a while for most players to make this an automatic reaction.

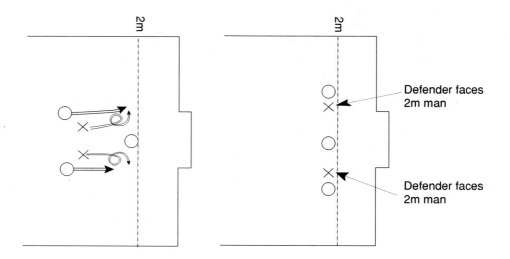

#62 SHOOTER CHASE DRILL

Objective: To improve defender's anticipation and execution of a counter after a shot.

Description: When an offensive player shoots, the defender on that player fakes a charge and then continues down court with the offensive shooter chasing. The break away player then receives a pass, either from the goalie or a designated passer.

Variation: The same drill can be run from the other end of the pool. The defender can begin on the outside or inside of the shooter, as determined by the coach.

Coaching Points:

- The offensive player should always be distracted, even if the defender cannot get close enough to actually block the shot. The concept to emphasize is that whatever happens, there should be a counter reaction.

- The chasers must keep moving until their head is between the driver and the goal.

- Chasers need to be aware that a foul within the four-meter area results in a penalty throw.

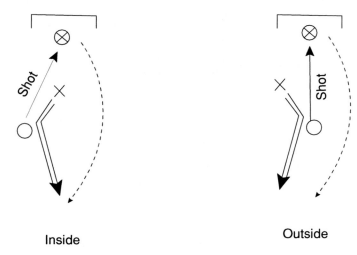

Inside   Outside

#63 WING PICK DEFENSE DRILL

Objective: To improve defensive skills by protecting the center of the field against offensive picks.

Description: This drill covers three different defensive maneuvers to practice against wing picks. The first maneuver is illustrated in Diagram A. The defender closest to the goal must identify the potential pick and slide back while turning his hips inward toward the goal. The second defender slides in, shoulder to shoulder with the first defender, essentially forming a wall. Both players make sure they are also in a passing lane, forcing the two-meter player with the ball to attempt a pass over their heads. This "wall" forces the pick away from the goal and into a less desirable shooting angle. The second technique is the best defensive solution, and is illustrated in Diagram B. Both defenders use proper body positioning to keep the offensive players from setting the pick. Diagram C illustrates what to do if a pick is successfully set. The defender closest to the goal calls for the switch and the outside defender drops in between the other defender's man and the goal. As this is happening, the defender who made the call switches to the player coming off the pick.

Variations: This drill can be run with the offense attacking at "walk-through" speed (50%) or at game speed (100%).

Coaching Points:

- Defenders must never allow an offensive player to drive down the center of the field of play. If a pick is set, the defenders must force the pick away from the center in order to give the goalie a better chance to block a shot taken from a less desirable shooting angle.

- Diagram C is the same for a two-meter switch, or an easy switch, when there is no danger of a quick pass to two meters.

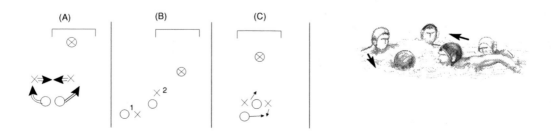

#64 FOUL THROUGH TO FRONT DRILL

Objective: To improve the two-meter defender's ability to move in front of the two-meter player and intercept or deflect a release pass.

Description: Drill begins with two offensive perimeter players, a two-meter player, and a two-meter defender. As illustrated in Diagram A, when a pass comes in from the point, the two-meter defender fouls through and moves in front of the two-meter player, who should attempt to pass out to the second perimeter player. After adding two perimeter defenders as illustrated in Diagram B, a pass is made to the two-meter player while the two-meter defender again fouls through to the ball side and the outside defenders press on the perimeter in an effort to protect against a back-door pass.

Variations: This drill can be run with the offense attacking at "walk-through" speed (50%) or at game speed (100%). This drill should be practiced with passes coming from both sides as well as the point. This drill can be run with a full contingent of offensive and defensive players.

Coaching Points:

- The two-meter defender should only foul through to the front of the two-meter player when the perimeter offensive players are beyond seven meters or the deep wings, closest to the goal, are being defended.

- A goalie who reads the offense correctly can intercept or defend a back door pass.

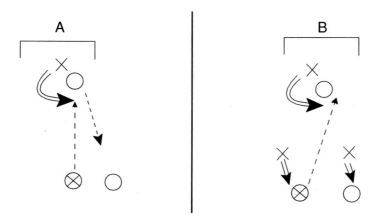

#65 ZONE DEFENSE DRILL

Objective: To improve team defense by practicing zone defense and counter-attacking out of a zone defense.

Description: This is a game situation drill that begins with four offensive and four defensive players. Defensive player one, guarding an offensive player with a bad angle, drops back to double team the two-meter player. Defensive player two, who is defending the center, shifts to a position between the two outside offensive players. Defensive player three must press his man. The offensive players on top look to pass to the two-meter player or shoot. Defense runs a five-stroke counterattack on any missed shot or turnover.

Variations: This drill can be run with any of the following variations:

Four-on-four half-court with the offense attacking at "walk through" speed (50%).

Four-on-four half-court with the offense attacking at game speed (100%).

Four-on-four full court with a counter and reset on the other end (100%).

Six-on-six half-court with the offense attacking at "walk through" speed (50%).

Six-on-six half-court with the offense attacking at game speed (100%).

Six-on-six full court with the offense attacking at game speed (100%).

Coaching Points:

- Player two should stunt back and forth between the two offensive players, taking the player closest to the cage or the player designated by the goalkeeper.

- Player three should move into position for a counterattack.

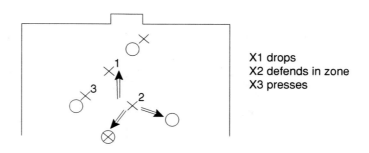

X1 drops
X2 defends in zone
X3 presses

#66 TEAM DROP TO ZONE DRILL

Objective: To improve team transition to defense while ensuring coverage of the most dangerous defensive positions and protecting the two-meter defender.

Description: Drill begins with six players set up in a 3-3 offense. On the whistle, they swim back to set up their defense. Three players go to the two-meter line, while two players pinch into a 3-2 defense. The center player (usually the two-meter player in a game) swims straight back to fill in the defense. From these positions, the players can either stay in the zone or switch to a man-to-man defense.

Variation: Once positioning becomes automatic, add defensive players at the beginning of the drill.

Coaching Point:

- All players must be aware of the position of the ball during transition. If they blindly swim back unaware of the position of the ball, the offensive team can get the ball down the court before the defenders can establish their proper positions.

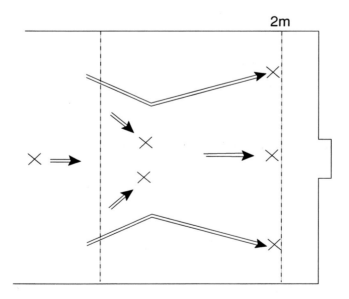

#67 KEEP AWAY DRILL

Objective: To improve individual and team defensive skills.

Description: Drill begins with three offensive players and two defenders within a two-and-a-half-meter square area (use lane lines, cones or other objects for boundary lines). The offensive players must stay within this area or they lose possession of the ball. If a defensive player steals the ball, that defender and the player who made the pass switch positions. If the ball hits the water, the defensive player closest to the ball goes on offense and the passer goes on defense.

Variation: The same drill can be run using a larger area and four or five offensive players and three or four defenders. This is a good team drill, with all of the defensive players going on offense at the same time when they get a turnover. The player not involved in the pass or reception, or the player farthest from the play, stays on offense.

Coaching Point:

- This should be a physical drill. The defense should be aggressive, using baiting and other tactics to keep the offense off balance.

2.5m

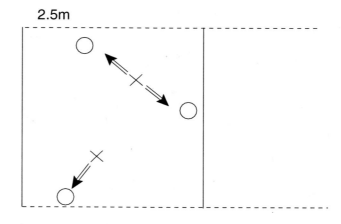

#68 FOUR-ON-FOUR CONTROLLED SCRIMMAGE DRILL

Objective: To improve quick decision-making and general defensive skills through highly competitive scrimmages.

Description: Scrimmage starts with a sprint from both ends of a 25-meter course.

Variations: Coach can set up a variety of scrimmage parameters, including: winners out (team that scores gets the ball back) and counterattack scrimmage (whether a team scores or not, there is an immediate counterattack). When quick ejections are added (player swims back and touches goal post and returns), opportunities for quick four-on-three situations arise.

Coaching Points:

- Four-on-four closely simulates situations, including team balance, that occur in a 30-meter course.

- This is an excellent conditioning drill, and exposes players to many important offensive and defensive frontcourt situations.

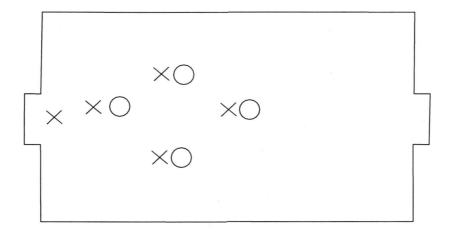

#69 NEAR-SIDE TANDEM DROP DRILL

Objective: To improve team defense through practice in dropping outside defenders back on the two-meter player.

Description: Beginning in a 3-3 formation, the outside perimeter defenders press their man and the defenders on the outside-point players drop back to inhibit a pass to the two-meter players. As those defenders drop back, the other outside defenders move between their man and the unguarded point players, making sure their original man cannot receive a pass. If the pass goes to a point player, then the defenders who were guarding the passers switch onto the point players until the original defenders come back out to cover them. The same switching takes place if the ball goes to the other side. The two-meter defenders must help the goalie by covering one part of the goal from any potential outside shooter.

Variations: Drill can be started at "walk through" speed (50%) until the defenders get used to the proper switching. Then run the drill at full speed, as a half-court controlled scrimmage.

Coaching Points:

- This drop-back technique gives the goalie a good opportunity to concentrate on the ball because he has to move the least distance to cover the shooters.

- This technique also eliminates many cross passes that have a higher chance of success.

- The drop-back player moves only to the right-hander's arm, to buy time, until the man-on-man defense is picked up.

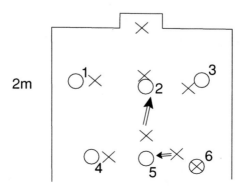

#70 ELEVEN AND ONE O'CLOCK DROP DRILL

Objective: To improve team defense through practice in dropping outside defenders back on the two-meter player.

Description: Drill begins in a 3-3 formation. When O^6 has the ball but his back is turned away from his two-meter player, then the defender on O^4 can look to drop to steal the ball. If O^4 has the ball in the same situation, then the defender on O^6 looks to drop.

Variations: Drill can be run at "walk through" speed and then as a full speed half-court controlled scrimmage.

Coaching Points:

- The eleven and one o'clock drops are dangerous because a cross-court pass puts the goalie in a disadvantageous situation. These drops can only be anticipated when the player with the ball has his back to his two-meter player.

- Steal attempts from the defenders on O^1 and O^3 must be successful because of the added danger of a quick pass.

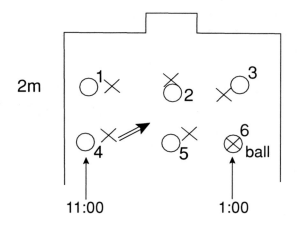

#71 CENTER PLAYER DROP DRILL

Objective: To improve team defense through practice in dropping outside defenders back on the two-meter player.

Description: Drill begins in a 3-3 formation. The defender on O^5 drops back and double teams the two-meter player. The defender on O^6 moves and reaches for the shooter, if right-handed. If the shooter is left-handed, the defender on O^4 reaches in with his left hand. At the same time, the two-meter defender raises one hand to help protect one side of the goal. Therefore, if a shot is taken, it is channeled toward one area that the goalie must cover.

Variations: Drill can be started at "walk through" speed (50%) until the defenders get used to the proper switching. Then run the drill at full speed, as a full court controlled scrimmage, resetting on each end.

Coaching Point:

- The defenders on O^4 and O^6 should be very mobile players due to the excellent angle for O^5.

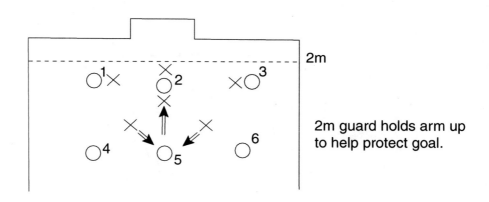

2m

2m guard holds arm up
to help protect goal.

#72 CRASH BACK DRILL

Objective: To improve team defense through practice at dropping outside defenders back on the two-meter player.

Description: Drill begins in a 3-3 formation, with three offensive players on the perimeter, a two-meter player, and three defenders on the perimeter. The ball is passed into the two-meter player, without interference, and all three defenders on the perimeter crash back onto the two-meter player. The two-meter player picks up the ball and passes out to any of the offensive perimeter players. The defenders who just crashed back stay in passing lanes, so when the two-meter player with the ball attempts to pass, it must be over the head of a defender.

Variations: Drill can be started at "walk through" speed (50%) until the defenders get used to the proper positioning. Then run the drill at full speed. The drill can also be run with a full contingent of players (six-on-six).

Coaching Points:

- This situation will occur when a team is caught off guard and there is an unequal situation at the two-meter position.

- If one of the outside perimeter players gets the ball, the defender rolls and turns to defend. If the defender cannot get to the player with the ball, the defender must keep his arm up and get higher and higher in the water, blocking the shooting area with his hand, arm and body.

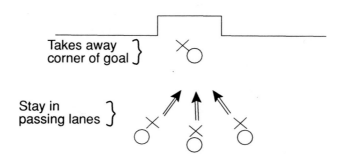

#73 LEFT-SIDE DOUBLE DROP DRILL

Objective: To improve team defense through practice at taking away easy access to the two-meter player and setting up a counterattack.

Description: Beginning in a 3-3 formation, the two defensive players on the outside of the goalie's left side drop off their players, inhibiting passes to the two-meter player, and encouraging the ball to go to these two positions. The other side of the defense pressures their opponents. If the ball is shot from one of these unguarded players, a counterattack is set up.

Variations: Drill can be started at "walk through" speed (50%) until the defenders get used to the proper positioning. Then run the drill at full speed, as a full court controlled scrimmage, resetting at each end

Coaching Points:

- Since most players are right handed, and are inclined to protect the ball with their left hand and pick up the ball with their right hand, they have a tendency to always go to their right. Taking this tendency into consideration, and adding the fact that a right-handed shooter on the goalie's left side has a poorer shot angle, there is a lower probability of the shooter making a goal from that position.

- Defenders must understand that if an outstanding shooter, particularly a left-handed one, is in that position, this defensive maneuver should be modified.

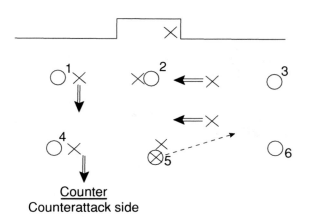

Counter
Counterattack side

#74 PRESS MAN-TO-MAN DRILL

Objective: To improve individual and team defensive skills through practice at setting up in proper frontcourt defensive positions.

Description: Drill begins with six defensive players and six offensive players set up in a 3-3 formation. The offense starts with their backs to the cage. Players go through every combination of two-meter defender positions and offensive ball positions to ensure each defender knows his responsibilities. The defense must be in perfect body position and in the passing lanes at all times, or the drill should be stopped and the mistake corrected.

Variations: Drill should be run as a "walk through" at first, so every player is reminded of the proper positions. Then run the drill at half-speed, and then at full-speed, always stopping and pointing out when a player is not in the correct position.

Coaching Points:

- When practicing set-ups and steals, the offensive players must "play along" for the drill to be effective, since the element of surprise is essential. The defensive player must make the offensive player believe he is going to steal the ball on the side of the "set-up."

- Rotate players into different positions as often as possible.

- If the ball is behind half-court the two-meter defender plays in front.

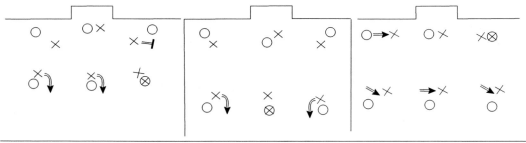

Reverse to opposite wing

When ball is at the point, defender takes the power side. (The strongest turn by offensive 2m man)

Reverse to opposite wing

#75 HALF-COURT, SIX-ON-SIX SYSTEM DRILL

Objective: To improve team defense by simulating game situations in a controlled scrimmage.

Description: Drill is a controlled, half-court scrimmage with a coach keeping score. When the defense gets five points, they switch to offense. When the offense gets to five points, they stay on offense. The defensive team gets a point for every steal and offensive foul, while the offensive team gets a point for every goal and ejection. The scrimmage begins when any of the offensive perimeter players, with their backs to the goal, put the ball in play.

Variation: Drill can be run as a six-on-five extra player situation. If the defense stops the offense, they get a point. If the offense scores, they get a point.

Coaching Points:

- Once a definitive offensive is determined, then the frontcourt offense and defense can be staged.

- Coach can start the drill with the ball in any position he wants to work on, for example, a corner throw or a free throw on the perimeter.

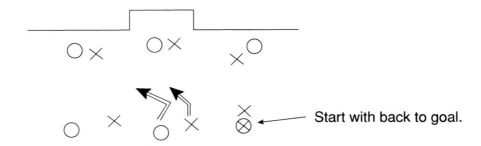

Start with back to goal.

CHAPTER 6

5-ON-6 DEFENSIVE DRILLS

Introduction

In the modern game of water polo, with different referee philosophies, the number of ejections in a game can become the primary reason for a team winning or losing. For example, in the Atlanta Olympics there were no natural goals scored in either of the semi-final games. The success of the 6-on-5 power plays and one penalty-throw decided the outcome of both games. There are three basic defensive schemes: Defending against the 3-3 and the 4-2 offensive formations, and defending the various rotations within each of these formations. All defensive players must be schooled in the basic defensive strategies and requirements. Defensive systems must be selected, practiced and learned. Every player must understand all facets of each position. It is imperative that the current 20-second ejection rule be explained. The placement of the defensive players in a 5-on-6 is crucial, especially when the opportunity affords itself, such as after a time out. With one less defender, the defensive players must stay alert by improving their concentration, anticipation and awareness of the situation. Scouting reports and videotapes are necessary in order to understand the 6-on-5 tendencies of the opponents. The following guidelines are for a proper five-on-six defense:

- Always be aware of the ejection in order to set up as quickly as possible.

- The defender should exit quickly, possibly causing the offense to take more time in determining what their options may be.

- Defenders should concentrate on looking for the opportunity to press the first pass. At times, this can throw the offensive team off balance during their attack.

- Learn to protect against the quick shot, and cover the back line first.

- Always be looking to intercept passes, press, or even foul and drop to keep the offensive team off balance.

- Prevent all passes to the posts.

- Match hand-to-ball (mirror) perimeter shooters.

- Watch the eyes of the player with the ball. Be aware of the direction he is looking. This will often give a hint as to where the pass is going.

When not specifically setting a defense to guard specific players, as determined by scouting, the following points may be helpful in determining defensive positions:

- A very effective defense can be set when the back-line defenders are mobile.

- The center defender must be able to cover both posts; help block outside shots; take away weak-side shots; and retrieve rebounds.

- The defender guarding the offensive player in the number one position must be quick enough to keep number two off balance and still charge the number one player. He must be able to protect the goal on rebound shots and still be a safety-release pass outlet if the goalie is attacked.

- The outside right defender must anticipate guarding the number four offensive player because that player has a better shooting angle and is in a better position to facilitate the movement of the ball in triangles. At key times, this defender can split the two offensive players on the perimeter and steal the ball.

O = Offense

X = Defense

$$O^1 \quad X^1 \quad O^2 \quad X^2 \quad O^3 \quad X^3 \quad O^6$$
$$X^4 \qquad X^5$$
$$O^4 \qquad O^5$$

X^1 — Ready to charge O^1, and take away the quick shot. Deny a pass from O^6 to O^2 when O^2 is inside of two meters. Communicate to X^4 if O^1 rotates up. Look for rebounds and be available for a release pass.

X^2 — Take away weak side pass from O^4 or O^5 to O^2 and O^3, and protect against an upper corner shot when weak side on O^2. Be aware of right side near triangles, keep O^3 off balance and help weak side on O^2, (depending on which defensive system is used). Look for rebounds, and on desperation, counterattack out.

X^3 — Take away near side shot by O^5. Keep O^3 off balance when O^1 has the ball. Communicate to X^5 if O^6 rotates up. Deny pass from O^6 to O^3. Be ready to charge O^6. Look for rebounds and release pass.

X^4 — When O^1 has the ball, position in the lane with regards to O^4's position. Look to split between O^4 and O^5 when offense rotates into a 3-3. Take away near corner shot when O^4 has ball. Look to blind side when O^6 has the ball, but return quickly to original formation after O^6 releases ball. Look to counterattack.

X^5 — Deny passes to O^3. During rotations, look to split between O^5 & O^6 when the offense moves into a 3-3. Look to counterattack.

#76 MIRROR DRILL

Objective: To improve individual defensive shot-blocking skills.

Description: Two players pair up, with the offensive player faking several times and then shooting. From a distance of approximately three meters, the defensive player keeps one hand up and mirrors the movement of the ball, attempting to block the shot.

Variations: Drill can be run with three or four partners and a goalie at each cage. Players shoot in order and then rotate from offense to defense. Another variation has five or six partners per cage without a goalie. This time the offensive players shoot at will, and then rotate to defense. This technique can also be incorporated into any five-on-six drill. Another variation has each defender keeping both hands up, one mirrors the ball while the other takes away the weak side shot.

Coaching Points:

- Defensive players must be as high as possible and keep their eye on the ball at all times. They must concentrate on the ball for this technique to be effective.

- This defense can be used on number four and number five offensive players.

#77 GAGE THE DISTANCE MOVEMENT DRILL

Objective: To improve team defense by learning to gage distances in order to charge an offensive player. This drill also helps players understand how to work together to cover a post player.

Description: Drill involves five players, three on offense and two on defense. The offensive players are positioned at the seven-meter line, the two-meter post and the two-meter line approximately three meters from the post. The two defensive players are positioned between the two-meter post player and each of the other offensive players. The defenders must work in unison in this drill. Beginning with defender one touching the seven-meter player and defender two touching the three-meter post player, the ball goes to the uncovered offensive player. Defender one then moves quickly to defend the two-meter post player and defender two, after waiting for his partner to touch the post player, moves quickly out to touch the player with the ball. When the ball is passed back to the seven-meter player, the sequence is reversed for the two defensive players. The drill continues with the defenders moving back and forth.

Variation: Drill can be run on both wings.

Coaching Points:

* This drill demands intensity and speed.

* Drill should only run 10 seconds and then the positions rotated.

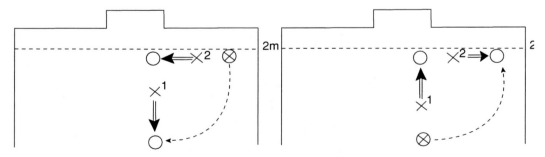

Pass from wing to top Player 1 swims and touches player with ball. Player 2 keeps hand on position.

Pass from top to wing. Player 2 swims and touches player with ball. Player 1 keeps hand on pos man.

Players do not leave until teammate touches offensive player.

#78 EUROPEAN SUICIDE DRILL

Objective: To intimidate offensive shooters by jamming back line defensive players in goal.

Description: Drill begins with the defensive back-line wing players dropping back in goal. The center defender moves forward, and the two outside defenders drop into position just back from the center defender. A defensive triangle is formed with the goalie as the base. The center defender can stunt toward a shooter to create bad shooting angles.

Variations: Defensive players should move out to guard from basic 4-2 or 3-3 positions and then back into the suicide positions. Wing players can use opposite crossover arm positions, but the center defender keeps both arms up and/or chases the shooter away from a center shot opportunity.

Coaching Points:

- This technique is used primarily by a few European teams, and is a dangerous technique because experienced players can just come in and shoot as hard as they can, usually just above head high.

- In practice sessions, it is better to stage this drill rather than run it at full intensity.

- Individual abilities of opponents must be scouted in order to avoid giving the shot to their best offensive players.

#79 BOTTOM-SLIDE DEFENSE FORMATION DRILL

Objective: To improve team defensive skills in a five-on-six situation.

Description: This drill helps players understand their responsibilities when the offense has a six-on-five ejection opportunity. With the offense set in a 4-2 formation, when O^6 has the ball, the bottom line slides towards the ball. The defender on O^5 helps guard O^3. The defender on O^4 slides into the passing lane between O^4 and O^5. The defender on O^2 slides between O^2 and the goal. When O^1 has the ball, the bottom line slides toward the ball. The defender on O^4 drops to help guard O^2, while the defender on O^5 splits. The defender on O^3 slides between O^3 and the goal.

Variations: Begin this drill as a "walk through" until the system is learned, then run it as a game speed drill, with the defenders on O^4 and O^5 matching hands (right hand up on left-handers and left hand up on right-handers).

Coaching Points:

- Emphasize that players must be ready to cover a wider area because they are a player short.

- Defenders must be able to read and anticipate who is going to receive the ball, and recognize the opponent's best shooters. They must know when they have a chance to steal the ball, or throw the offense off rhythm in order to give the goalie a better chance to block a shot.

- If O^1 or O^6 passes the ball outside, defenders drop back into the 3-2 formation.

#80 OPPOSITE-POST DEFENSE DRILL

Objective: To improve team defensive skills when the offense has a six-on-five ejection opportunity.

Description: This drill helps players understand their responsibilities when the offense has a six-on-five ejection opportunity. With the offense set in a 4-2 formation, when O^6 has the ball, the defender on O^5 drops to help guard O^3 while the defender on O^4 slides into the passing lane between O^4 and O^5. The defender covering O^2 pretends to be guarding O^3, but protects against a pass to O^2. When O^1 has the ball, the movement is the same to that side.

Variation: Once the positioning is learned, then emphasize that the defenders keep their hand up, matching the hands of O^4 and O^5 (right hand up against left-handers, and left hand up against right-handers).

Coaching Points:

- Emphasize that players must be ready to cover a wider area because they are a player short.

- Defenders must be able to read and anticipate who is going to receive the ball, and recognize the opponent's best shooters. They must know when they have a chance to steal the ball, or throw the offense off rhythm in order to give the goalie a better chance to block a shot.

#81 FIVE-ON-SIX COUNTER DRILL

Objective: To improve team defensive skills by practicing transitions from a player-down defense into a counter out.

Description: Drill begins with the offense set up in a 4-2 extra-player formation. The defense sets up in a 3-2. On the coach's whistle, the offensive player who has the ball shoots. The defense counters out the top two players, with defender one countering strong then making a sharp hook to get the offensive player on him to follow him out. At the same time, the defender from the center position drives directly down the court while the other outside defender also drives, creating a two-on-one in front of the goal. The defensive goalie should have an extra ball ready in order to facilitate a counter pass in case the ball that was shot is not available.

Variation: Drill can be run with a counter out on the opposite side.

Coaching Points:

- This is a risky counter move because countering with the center defensive player leaves the goal unguarded. This is a desperation play to be used if a goal attempt is absolutely necessary.

- This counter is not as effective from a 3-3 formation.

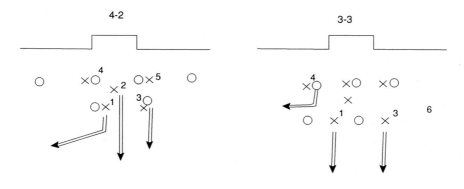

#82 COMBO DRILL

Objective: To improve team pressure-defense and counterattack skills.

Description: Drill begins with one team on offense and one on defense, set up in a six-on-five situation. The defensive team has a sixth player off to the side, on the two-meter line. If the offensive team scores, they stay on offense. If they miss the shot, the defensive team counters using the extra player as their sixth player. After the counterattack down to the goal, play is stopped and the defenders set up as the offensive team and the offensive team (with their sixth player off to the side on the two-meter line) sets up on defense, ready to counterattack back the other way.

Variation: Drill can be effective in both a 30-meter and 25-meter course.

Coaching Points:

- Each team should be given five minutes to prepare.

- This is a good drill for team members to get used to communicating with each other.

- Use a variety of defensive systems.

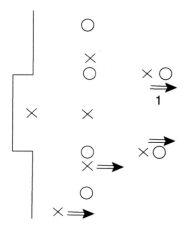

Counterattack

CHAPTER 7

GOALIE DRILLS

Introduction

No position in water polo demands that a player be secure in their position more than the goalkeeper position. The goalkeeper is the last line of defense for a team. The last picture a losing team will see is the ball going past their goalkeeper into the goal. The player in the goalie position can make or break a team's morale and confidence. In fact, the ability to successfully counterattack is often based on the confidence a team has in their goalie. Many mediocre teams with a good goalkeeper have beaten teams with better players but a weaker goalie.

The goalie has the responsibility of directing the team in both its defensive and offensive efforts. Many times the goalie will be the one to tell the defensive players who to guard, or when to drop back, or press. Along with the mental requirements necessary to take the pressure of the position and the responsibility to help direct the team, there are physical requirements that a coach looks for in a goalkeeper. Among the physical characteristics desired are quick reflexes, excellent body balance, good physical size, the ability to pass the ball accurately, good lateral movement in the water, and great anticipation. A goalkeeper should be able to maintain a strong eggbeater kick for balance, as well as produce a powerful thrust with both legs, combined with a good kicking down motion at the same time, in order to reach out to block or catch a ball that has been shot at the goal.

The attributes and skill level of a team's goalie will ultimately help the coach determine what type of defense to play. Some goalkeepers defy the basic fundamental principles of the position, yet they are successful. The following illustrations show the basic positions for goalies for different types of shots. However, it is up to each coach to develop the team defense and the 5-on-6 defense that will give their goalie the best opportunity to stop the ball.

Goalies must know the game; they can be the coach in the water. They must understand a number of situations, for example, "stealing" the ball from the two-meter player when he has the ball and no outlet pass.

Goalkeepers must learn what to expect from the opposing team. They should know ahead of time the types of shots different players like to take, and anticipate when they might shoot. The goalies must also know the abilities of their own teammates. The goalie can sometimes determine the tempo of the game, and must have a good knowledge of the team's system of play.

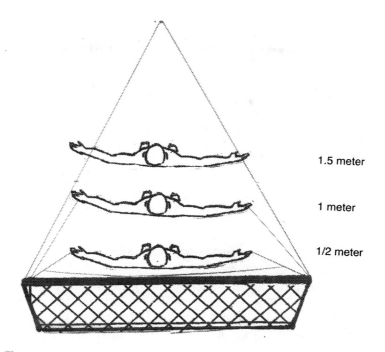

Angles for covering the goal from a shot from a distance

1.5 meter

1 meter

1/2 meter

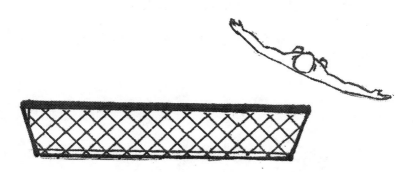

A shooter that is one on the goalie from the right.

Anticipation of a low shot on the water, the goalie backs up in the goal.

Shooter is on the goalie's far left side forcing only a high shot.

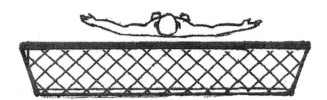

Anticipating a straight shot on the goal during regular front court offense.

Protecting from a deep left shooter.

Protecting from a deep right-handed shooter.

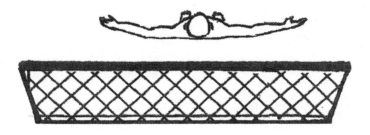

Ready for a high shot from further out.

#83 GOALIE SWIMMING STYLE DRILL

Objective: To practice specific swimming drills designed for goalkeepers.

Description: Goalies should practice the following swimming drills:

Dribble a short distance using a flutter kick, then switch to a high eggbeater kick, then a breast stroke kick. Pick up the ball, holding it high so receiver can see it, then pass the ball.

Swim all out for 25- or 30-meters using short strokes, then rest before repeating the drill. Goalies must keep their head up while using the butterfly, backstroke, breaststroke and crawl stroke.

Practice stop-and-go drills with the rest of the team.

Coaching Point:

  • Use the goalies to lead the field players in leg drills.

#84 SIDE TO SIDE DRILL

Objective: To improve the goalkeeper's awareness of the size of the goal.

Description: Begin with the goalie facing the goal. On the whistle, the goalie moves side to side, at water level, touching the posts of the goal as many times as possible in 10 seconds. Repeat this exercise three times.

Variation: Same drill with the goalie touching the upper corners of the goal while moving side to side.

Coaching Points:

- Coach should count the number of touches.

- Depending on the skill of the goalie, the coach can increase the time limit to 15 seconds.

#85 ABOVE GOAL DRILL

Objective: To improve the goalkeeper's awareness of the size of the goal.

Description: Begin with the goalie facing the goal, one yard away from it. The goalie moves across the cage and at each end, comes up with his head higher than the horizontal bar of the goal. This movement is repeated four times in each direction.

Variation: Same drill, but the goalie comes up and extends his hands over the top of the goal. Repeat four times form left to right and four times from right to left.

Coaching Points:

- Coach should monitor to make sure the goalie comes up and actually gets over the top bar of the goal.

- Encourage competition between goalies on all goalie drills.

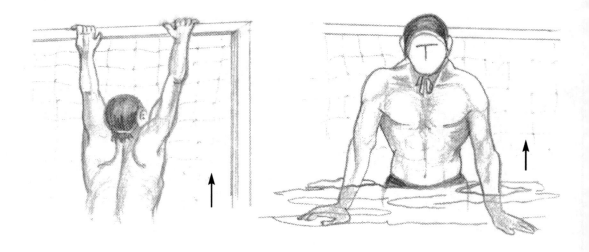

#86 TURNS DRILL

Objective: To improve the goalkeeper's quickness and conditioning.

Description: On the first whistle, the goalies come up in the water, and stays up. On the second whistle, they make quarter turns to the right until they circle back to the starting position. On the last whistle, they come up as high as they can and then drop down into the water. The drill is ten-seconds long, and repeats with the goalies turning to the left.

Variations: Same drill with the goalies making half-turns. Three-quarter turns and full circles are two other variations. As each turn is concluded, the goalies should remain high out of the water to use up the remainder of the ten-second time limit.

Coaching Points:

- Goalies should have a short rest between each 10-second drill.
- Emphasize coming up in the water before beginning the turns.

#87 FOUR-WHISTLE UP DRILL

Objective: To improve the goalkeeper's body control, conditioning and leg strength.

Description: Drill is run for ten seconds at a time. The first whistle signals the goalies to come up in the water. On the second whistle, they come up farther out of the water and extend their arms out to their sides. On the third whistle, they slowly come down until stopping on the fourth whistle. This drill is repeated four times with a short rest between each repetition.

Variation: Run the same drill with the goalie's hands remaining in the water.

Coaching Points:

- Encourage even more intensity on every drill

- Goalies must be able to show their swimsuit at the waist when they come up high in the water.

- Over the course of a practice, goalies should show their suit at least 300 times.

#88 TWENTY-FIVE METER WALK DRILL

Objective: To improve the goalkeeper's body control and leg strength.

Description: The goalie uses an eggbeater kick while "walking" for 25 or 30 meters. The goalie's arms must be kept straight up from the shoulders, with absolutely no head or arm movement.

Variations: Same drill with the goalie sculling with his arms and using an egg-beater kick. The drill can also be run with the goalie sculling forward or sideways for the first 25 meters, and then sculling backwards or sideways for the same distance in the other direction.

Coaching Point:

- Demand that the goalies keep their arms up with the elbows straight, even hyperextended, with no movement.

#89 LOB DRILL

Objective: To improve the goalkeeper's defensive technique against lob shots.

Description: Drills begins with players shooting lob shots from both wings, while the goalie protects the goal. When a lob shot is taken, the backhand of the goalie (farthest from the shooter)plants and stabilizes the body, while the near hand and arm are raised to catch or tip the ball.

Variation: Shooters can vary their shots to include near side shots at three-quarter speed.

Coaching Points:

- Few lob shots are taken during most games.

- Because the goalie's movement needs to be away from the shooter in order to intercept the lob shot on its downward movement, the shot must be correctly read by the goalie.

- Moving away from an incoming shot is the wrong technique in all other instances of shot blocking.

#90 HIGH-AND-LOW SHOT BLOCK DRILL

Objective: To improve the goalkeeper's ability to block open shots.

Description: This is a quick reflex drill that begins with two shooters lined up two meters outside the posts of the goal, on the three meter line , with a passer between them at seven meters. The goalie starts lined up on the passer. The passer passes the ball to either shooter, who catches the ball and quickly takes a shot. At first, shots are taken at three-quarter speed near the corners of the cage. Later, shooters can shoot either high or low. The proper technique for goalies is for them to reach down near the corner with their outside hand and arm, while their other hand and arm are positioned up near the center of the goal.

Variation: Slowly increase the velocity of the shots.

Coaching Point:

- The goalies need to position their head as close to the ball's line of flight as possible.

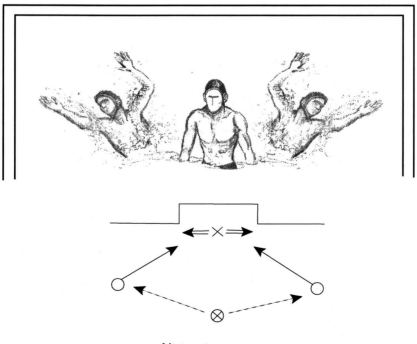

Alternate passes

#91 TWO SHOT BLOCK DRILL

Objective: To improve the goalkeeper's reactions and movement.

Description: Two shooters set up on the six-meter line, one on the right post and the other on the left post. On the whistle, and while shooting at three-quarter speed, the first shooter takes a shot on the water towards the near left post. On the second whistle, the second shooter takes a shot on the water towards the near right post. Each shooter has three balls, and they alternate shooting at the corners. The goalie slides laterally to protect the goal.

Variations: Same drill with the shooters aiming toward the top corners of the goal. Add a third shooter in the middle if desired. Another variation is to use drive-in shots.

Coaching Point:

- Control the timing of the shots to make the drill as realistic as possible.

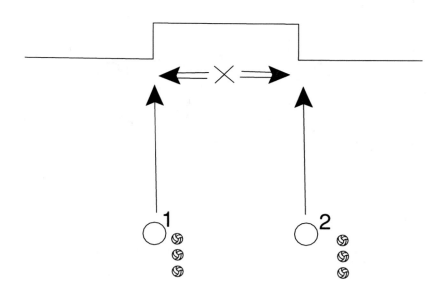

#92 GOALIE PASSING OPTIONS DRILL

Objective: To improve the goalkeeper's passing accuracy by practicing various types of passes from various distances.

Description: The following drills provide examples of game-situation passes a goalie needs to perfect:

Short passes to players making right and left wings. Field players drive center then hook at half-court (Diagram A).

Long passes to lead break after dribbling out to pass. Field players, from half-court, drive toward the opponent's goal, and receive the ball between the five-meter and three-meter lines (Diagram B).

Wet passes to safe areas. Guarded players drive from half-court and the goalie throws a wet pass to the side of the driver away from the defender (Diagram C).

Two-hand passes. A field player shoots a staged three-quarter speed shot over the goalie's head, and the goalie catches the shot with two hands and quickly releases to the breaking player, five-meters away (Diagram D).

Coaching Point:

- The goalie is the field general. He must make good, quick decisions as well as accurate passes.

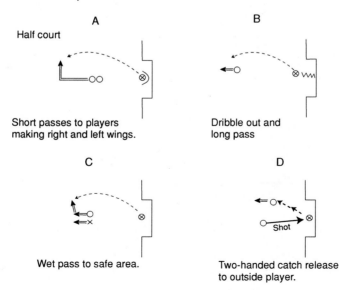

127

#93 SHOOT-ON-THE-WHISTLE DRILL

Objective: To improve the goalkeeper's ability to time shots, prepare to block shots, and react to the position of the shooter.

Description: Two lines are formed at the outside wing positions. The first player in line one dribbles in, and on the coach's whistle, rears up and shoots. Then the first player from the other line does the same thing. The two lines alternate driving and shooting.

Variation: Same drill, only this time when the whistle blows, the player with the ball shoots immediately or passes to a player in the second line, who shoots immediately.

Coaching Point:

- Coach should count the number of times the goalie touches the ball.

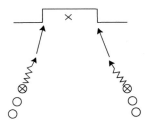
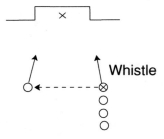

#94 HEAD AND TWO-HAND PULL DOWN DRILL

Objective: To improve the goalkeeper's ability to properly line up with the ball.

Description: Drill begins with a teammate on the four-meter line passing the ball at half speed toward the goalie. The goalie returns the ball to the passer using a soccer style "header."

Variation: From the six-meter line, a player shoots over the goalie's head at three-quarter speed. The goalie catches the ball with both hands over the top of the ball, thumbs almost touching, and pulls the ball down with both hands.

Coaching Points:

- Emphasize that the goalie lines up with the shooter's arm and hand, not his head.

- This is an important drill to help the goalie line up properly with the ball.

- The goalie's elbows must be high.

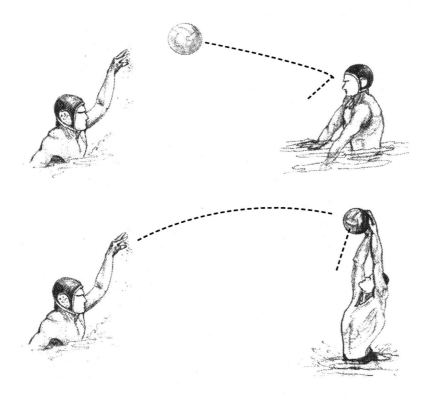

#95 TWO-METER SHOT BLOCKING DRILL

Objective: To improve the goalkeeper's positioning skills and shot-blocking ability.

Description: Drill begins with a passer on the four-meter line and a two-meter player facing away from the goal. The goalies put their hands up as the ball is passed to the two-meter player, who shoots a variety of hole shots at half speed. Since the shot will often be a deflection shot, the goalies use their body to stay in line with the ball.

Variation: Same drill can be run with the addition of a two-meter defender. The defender sets up in different positions on the shooter.

Coaching Point:

- Because goalies cannot usually see the origin of shots, their body position becomes even more important.

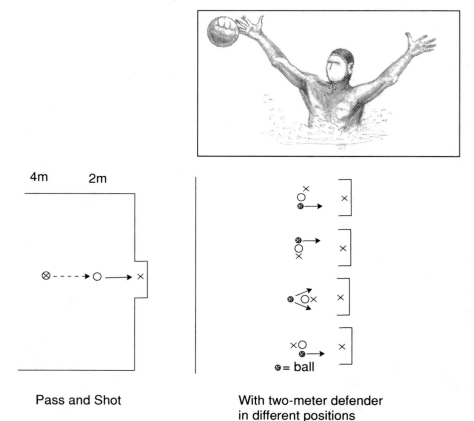

| Pass and Shot | With two-meter defender in different positions |

#96 FIVE-ON-SIX MOVEMENT DRILL

Objective: To improve the goalkeeper's movement when down a player in an extra player situation.

Description: Two players on opposite wings along the three-meter line pass the ball back and forth until the whistle blows. The player with the ball shoots at the goal.

Variation: Shooting speeds and locations can be staged.

Coaching Point:

- All goalies will have slightly different methods of moving across goal and the angles they defend. However, the basic concept is to use the hands and feet to move across the goal, and the legs to help get the hands up, or help the goalie come up in water and block shots.

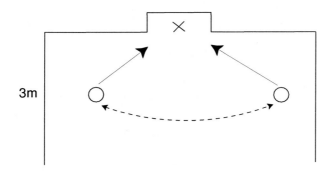

#97 PERIMETER OFFENSIVE POSITION DRILL

Objective: To improve the goalkeeper's ability to defend against shots coming from the outside.

Description: Drill begins with three offensive players outside the six-meter line, passing the ball back and forth and taking shots. The goalies use their hands and feet to move across goal, following the passes. They pull their hands out of the water to defend against the shots.

Variation: Add two defenders between the three shooters to simulate the perimeter offense of a 3-3 formation. If the defenders intercept a pass, the passer and the intended receiver switch to defense.

Coaching Point:

- This is a good drill for practicing a six-on-five shooting defense, and a 3-3 formation against a drop back that is part of a frontcourt offense.

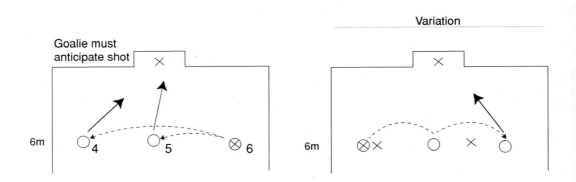

#98 PENALTY SHOT DRILL

Objective: To improve the goalkeeper's confidence in his ability to block penalty shots.

Description: Drill begins with the goalie setting up in a proper goal position, and three field players taking turns shooting penalty shots on the whistle.

Variation: Position another player behind the goal, and after each penalty shot is taken, that player throws another ball over, and in front of, the goal. The shooter and the goalie try to get control of the staged rebound. (Ignore where the shot goes.)

Coaching Points:

- This drill presents the ultimate goalie challenge. Prior to each shot, the goalies should exaggerate their size by laying out wide and coming up extra high in the water.

- Goalies should occasionally make movements toward the shooter.

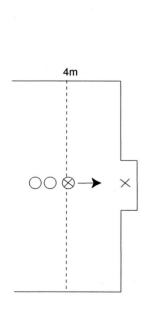

#99 CHALLENGE DRILL

Objective: To improve the goalkeeper's confidence by challenging the field players to try to score.

Description: Drill begins with ten to twelve players, each with a ball, lining up on the seven-meter line. One at a time, on the whistle, they hold up their ball so the goalie can see it, and on the whistle they then shoot. Shooting continues left to right, and then back right to left.

Coaching Points:

- Be sure that players shoot one at a time.
- This drill helps goalie with body positioning.
- This is a good drill to do before a game.

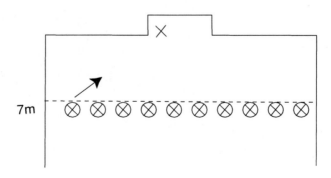

#100 THREE-SHOT WHISTLE DRILL

Objective: To improve the goalkeeper's reactions against three different shots.

Description: Drill is set up with two players lined up on the three-meter line, one-and-a-half meters outside the posts. Another player is located on the four-meter line in the penalty-throw position. Two other players are lined up on the seven-meter line. The three-meter and seven-meter players continuously pass their balls back and forth. On the first whistle, the player with the ball on the seven-meter line shoots at goal. On the second whistle, the three-meter player with the ball shoots. On the third whistle, the player on the four-meter line shoots a penalty throw.

Variation: The first shot can come from the player on the three-meter line or the four-meter line. The sequence of shots can be varied.

Coaching Point:

• This drill is best run under the coach's supervision.

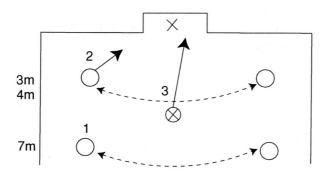

#101 BACK-DOOR DEFENSE DRILL

Objective: To improve the goalkeeper's skills against a back door by the two-meter player.

Description: Drill sets up with six players, three on offense, two on defense, and a goalie. The two-meter player makes a back door move on the defensive player that is fronting him. The goalie moves to take away the long pass, while the wing defender drops in to help.

Variation: This should first be run as a staged drill with only passing. Then it can be run as in a game situation with defenders on the passers, who can pass or shoot depending on the situation.

Coaching Points:

- The two-meter back door move occurs frequently when the two-meter player is being fronted, therefore all of the defensive players should be aware of the possibility of this move when they are in this situation.

- The potential back door should be called out by the goalie.

- The goalie must not give up the strong side shot to help defend back door. He can help after a foul (inside seven meters) or when teammates are pressing.

- The two-meter defender should stay close to the two-meter player, but avoid being ejected. The defender should turn to face the pass and hold up one hand to inhibit or intercept the pass.

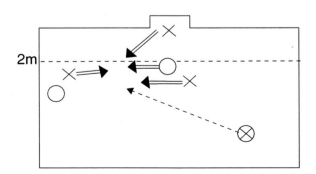

THE COACH:

All coaches must develop their own philosophy about coaching; their own set of guidelines and direction for their teams. There are a lot of areas to ponder in the development of a team. The following ideas and credos represent some of the information that we have accumulated over the years that we feel every coach should consider:

- Determine the purpose of the team. Try to imbue to each player "a sense of honor, genuine team spirit and respect for the opponent."

As a coach:

- Enjoy the challenge.
- Be willing to spend the time to learn.
- Winning is a worthy goal, but by no means the only criteria for playing the game.
- The journey is the most important thing, the championship is the by-product of improvement.
- Be your own personality.
- Work on communication with the players.
- Have team meetings, and don't be afraid to say, "I don't know."
- Understand that you, as a coach, have never thrown a ball, never won a sprint, never scored a goal or blocked a shot or made a pass.
- When in doubt, go back to fundamentals.
- When you have a good team, the players take responsibility.
- Understand that discontent is the first step toward progress.
- Be willing to experiment early in the season or in the off-season.
- Plan the season. Make lesson plans for each training session.
- In the history of the world, no one has ever built a monument to a critic.
- What a team needs from the coach is a chance to become better players, to be prepared, treated with fairness and the opportunity to compete.

BUILDING A TEAM

The Players:

- More than winning, a player wants to play.

- When dealing with the players on the bench, encourage them to put in the extra time and effort needed to improve. Work on their pride, their effort, and their value to the team. When possible, have the best player on the team not start.

- Sometimes you will have players who like each other, and sometimes you will have players who dislike each other. Certainly the former is more desirable. However, it is more important that the players respect each other's ability, and play with that in mind.

- Never praise personality, only performance. Criticize performance or errors, but never personality. Make sure the players understand the difference.

The Team:

- The only time to talk about winning is during the first team meeting.

- Always continue to try to determine what needs to be done to improve. Review weight training, swimming, drills, etc.

- Instill the thought and principle that the team must be greater than the sum of its parts.

- Rules and regulations – as a team, be at all practice sessions and be on time - the rest will be handled individually.

- In team meetings, all questions are good questions.

- Avoid cutting the team.

- The schedule, the competition, the opponents, the system of play – all should be clear and concise.

- For team development, schedule teams that are better and more experienced, teams that are equal and teams that are not as competitive.

- Expect to be competitive with everyone – accept no excuses.

- Do not bad mouth an opponent, rather rise to the occasion and accept the challenge. (Other teams probably work just as hard.)

- Offense is inconsistent by nature, but defense is hustle, concentration and consistency.

- No one quits, but sometimes players lose heart. If the team cannot win the game, win three-fourths of the game, if they can't win that much, then win half, or a quarter, or even one situation, and then build on that success. Something can be always be learned.

- Give 80% all of the time. Never lower than 80%. And at times the team will reach 100% - in practice and in games.

GAME GUIDELINES:

When there is a short time left in a game and your team is ahead and has the ball:

- If no shot is needed, protect the ball. Players make themselves available to receive a pass. It is best not to pass to a teammate coming towards the player with the ball.

- Do not allow any inside water drives. The goalie's leadership is vital, listen to his directions.

- Be aware of the 35-second clock. If a shot is needed, shoot high, after checking that all teammates are between their man and your goal.

- As the ball changes to the other team, all players must be between the player they are guarding and their own goal, protecting so that an opponent cannot swim down the center of the court.

- Do not let any offensive players swim down without being guarded (go back with the cherry picker).

- Play high water polo. Do not expect the referee to help in calling a foul. Protect the ball at all costs.

When there is a short time left in a game and your team is ahead, but on defense:

- If in man-to-man, position your players so that the offensive player turns his back on the offensive end of the court.
- Press the ball – all other players should give room and not permit inside drives.
- Try to make effective lunge blocks and grab blocks.
- Protect against desperation gross and go. Keep hips up, pointing toward your own goal.
- If the ball is shot, do not counterattack. All players must turn immediately to receive the ball.
- Watch the ball at all times.

When you are behind by one goal, with the ball, and there is a short time left in the game:

- Make sure you are in constant motion.
- Attempt to beat man on the offensive end.
- Be ready to attack the goalie, look for rebounds of shots taken.
- Try to make screens or picks with a teammate.
- Keep your eye on the ball at all times.
- Pass and go.
- Make yourself available to receive the ball.
- Gross and go (last resort).
- Take a strategic time out if one is available.
- Anticipate, anticipate, anticipate.

When you are behind by one goal, without the ball, with a short time left in the game.

- Press the ball all over the court.
- Bother every pass, and if time is a factor, foul to stop the clock.
- Get in the passing lanes and bait passes.
- Attempt to steal the ball every time there is an opportunity.
- Try to cheat up on the weak side.
- Counter on every shot.
- Cherry pick on the outside point position.
- Goalie should look to come out on long passes to try to steal the ball.
- Be ready to call a time out if your team gets possession of the ball.
- Keep your opponent static and low in the water.
- If a player has a free throw, stay very close.
- Constantly try to beat your man with inside water.

.

List of Terms

Back Door: An offensive drive from the wing position on the weakside (away from the ball).

Backhand Shot: Shot toward the goal while facing away from the goal.

Balance: While in a vertical position, keeping the body steady so a pass can be received or a shot taken with accuracy.

Ball Control: Offensive team maintains possession of the ball.

Body Fake: In passing, using the chest and upper body rotation so the pass looks like a shot.

Breakaway: When a player completely breaks away from the defense.

Cage: Another name for the water polo goal.

Circle Pass Drills: A series of passing drills with players formed in a circle.

Counter Rotate: During a counterattack, movement by players rotating away from the ball.

Counterattack: A fast break with players switching from defense to offense.

Crashing: Perimeter defenders dropping back quickly on a two-meter player with the ball.

Cross-face Pass: Ball is received across the face of a player.

Cross Over Backhand Pass/Shot: Rolling a hand over the ball and passing or shooting while facing away from the receiver or the goal.

Drive: An effort to swim past the defensive player.

Drive-in Shots: Shots taken by the driver.

Drop Back Defense: A zone or man-to-man defense where defensive players drop back off of the offensive perimeter players.

Dry Pass: Pass from one player to another without the ball touching the water.

Dribble: To swim with the ball in front of one's face, using the crawl arm stroke to keep the ball.

Eggbeater: An alternating breaststroke type of kick.

Ejection: When a player is removed for committing a major foul.

Eleven O'Clock: Far left outside position in a 3-3 formation.

Eye-to-Eye Contact: Offensive players looking directly at each other before a pass is made.

Eternity Drills: A drill that can be extended for an indefinite period of time.

Extra-man: An ejection (personal foul) of a player that enables the offensive team to have an extra player advantage, (6-on-5). Also, player up situations: two on one, three on two, etc.

Face-off: Like a jump ball, the official tosses a ball between offensive and defensive players who each attempt to gain possession of the ball.

FINA: Federation Internationale de Natation Amateur: An international governing aquatic body for diving, synchronized swimming, swimming and water polo.

Five-on-Six: The defensive line-up when a team has lost a player.

Forcing the ball: Trying to pass the ball past a defender or into an area that is being guarded.

Foul and Drop: When a defensive player commits a foul to slow play so he can drop back to defend an offensive player closer to the goal.

Four-two (4-2): The line-up for attacking a five-player defense, including extra-player and counterattack.

Front Court (Ft): The offensive half of the playing field (pool).

Front Water: When an offensive player has no defender between him and the defensive goal.

Gareeni Shot: A ball that is caught and immediately shot without noticeable body movement by the shooter.

Goalie or Goal Keeper: A designated player who defends the goal.

Grab Block: While an offensive player with the ball is in the process of passing, the defender grabs him around the waist and pulls him underwater and toward the defender.

Hesitation Drive: An attempt to get the defensive player off balance so a drive can be made.

High Water Polo: Pertains to alertness, staying high in the water.

Hole: Area in front of the cage.

Holeman: The player in the hole area (usually the two-meter player).

Hook: The act of turning – usually refers to right-angle moves or bow outs.

Hungarian Drill: A 6-on-5 drill devised by the Hungarian National Team.

Intensity Shooting Drills: Drills that involve extreme physical effort in regard to multiple shots by one person.

Inside: Offensive player gets in front of the defender.

Inside Water: Anywhere in the pool where an offensive player is ahead of the defender.

Kick Out: An ejection.

Lanes: Areas free of defenders arms, allowing safe passes, and/or areas into which defensive players move.

Layout Shot: Laying flat on one's back and shooting, (can also be a method of passing).

Lead Break: The players that reach the offensive end first.

Lunge Block: Matching hands of passer and pushing down.

Match Hands: Right to left – left to right matching of defender's hands to the shooters.

Mobility Drills: Drills that include movement and swimming.

Moving Pick: Moving screen intended to free an offensive player for a release pass and/or shot.

Natural Goals: Goals scored when both teams have an even number of play-ers.

Off Water Shot: A shot that is taken from the water.

Offensive Foul: Foul committed by an offensive player.

One O'Clock: Far right outside position in a 3-3 formation.

Pass and Go: Player passes then immediately drives.

Passing Lanes: Clear passing areas between offensive players.

Penalty Shot: Free shot at goal from the four-meter line.

Perimeter Passing: Usually refers to passing during a 6-on-5 situation or against a zone.

Pick: An offensive move to screen defenders away from the shooter.

Point: The position at the top of the offensive set-up in the center of the pool.

Pop Shot: Player lifts the ball with one hand and shoots the ball into the goal with the other hand.

Pull Back: An ejection foul when an offensive player, who is beating his defender, is pulled back by the defender.

Pump Ball: Faking as if to shoot.

Quicks: Referring to quick shots.

RB: Player stops quickly and rears up and back to receive the ball.

Rear Back: Same as RB.

Roll-and-Pass: Body rolls in a layout position, right to left or left to right.

Screw-shot: A drive-in shot using one hand to reach under the ball and, while rotating the wrist, bring the ball up to the shoulder and shoot.

Second Pass Counterattack: Lead break gets to the two-meter line while a pass is made to the half-court player who then passes to the lead break player.

Seesaw Passing: Coming up high in the water to receive the ball and again to pass the ball.

Sequential Wings: The timing of passes to players who are making wings to advance the ball.

Six-on-Five: A one-player advantage situation.

Stop-and-go: Attempting to get free from a player by stopping and going.

Strongside: The side of the pool where the ball is located.

Switch: Defenders switching defensive responsibilities.

Team Balance: An offensive formation for a team that enables it to successfully run its offense.

Three-three (3-3): Three players along the two-meter line and three players usually between the five- and six-meter line. Counterattack or extra player offense.

Timing Pass: Pass thrown in rhythm with another player, so he does not have to stop swimming or moving.

Transition: Going from defense to offense, or offense to defense.

Triangle: Offensive formation for a counterattack or for right or left 6-on-5 formations.

Triangle Passing: Referring to a 6-on-5 formation and the direction of passes on the perimeter.

Turn-over: Losing the ball to the other team.

Two-meter Defender: The guard on the two-meter player.

Two-meter Player: Holeman/player in front of the goal, who is the center of the offense.

Two-meter Shots: Shots taken by the two-meter player.

Two-meter Line: The line at each end of the pool where the offensive player is not allowed, unless the ball is inside or the player himself takes the ball into that area.

Walk: Pertains to players in drills using the eggbeater kick to go across the pool.

Weakside: The side of the pool away from the ball.

Wet Pass: A pass from one player to another that lands in the water near the receiver.

Wet Shot: A shot that is attempted while the ball is controlled in the water. This is also called an off the water shot.

Wing: Players position on each side of pool, front court or goal.

Zone Defense: Either a five-player zone against a six-player offense or a six-player zone defense.

25m: 25-meter pool length (women's field of play).

30m: 30-meter pool length. Also, the official length for high school, college and international water polo.

Peter J. Cutino Sr. is the all-time winningest coach, combined with NCAA and United States club championships, in the history of the sport of water polo in the United States. In his illustrious career, his teams won twenty-one national championships, including eight NCAA Championships (the most in NCAA water polo history).

A graduate of California State Polytechnic University in San Luis Obispo, where he was an outstanding athlete in three sports (water polo, swimming, and basketball), Peter began his renowned coaching career as the head swimming and water polo coach at Oxnard (CA) High School in 1957. In six seasons, his swimming teams won two California Interscholastic Federation Championships, five league championships, and sixty dual meets in a row. Concurrently, his water polo teams compiled an 87-8 record during that period.

In 1963, Peter was head varsity swimming and water polo coach at the University of California – Berkeley. Subsequently, he spent eleven years as the mentor of the swimming program. He served as the water polo coach for 26 seasons. During his tenure, his water polo teams accorded a remarkable 519 – 172 record. In the process, Peter was named "Water Polo Coach of the Year" on fifteen occasions by a distinguished array of collegiate, national, and international organizations. His coaching achievements are further reflected in the fact that he has been named to seven different athletic-related Halls of Fame, including The National Water Polo Hall of Fame in 1995. Perhaps his greatest honor occurred when the award given annually to the best men's and women's intercollegiate water polo player was named the Pete Cutino Award (the equivalent of the Heisman Trophy and the Wooden Award in football and basketball, respectively).

Peter and his wife, Louise, currently reside in Monterey, California. They have three grown children – Paul Joseph, Peter John, and Anna Marie.

Peter Cutino Jr. is currently an architect with G.T.P. Consultants in Seville, Spain. He is a 1984 graduate of the University of California, Berkeley, where he had a distinguished career as a water polo player. A two-time All-American on the Bears' water polo team, he helped lead Cal to the NCAA National Championship in 1983. In the process, he earned several honors, including being named Pac-10 Conference Player of the Year, NCAA Collegiate Co-Player of the Year, and co-MVP of the NCAA Tournament. As an athlete, he frequently participated in international competition in water polo during the period 1980 – 1987.

Peter began his coaching career in 1979, working as an age group coach for the Concord Water Polo Club. Beginning in 1984, he served as an assistant coach for his alma mater's water polo team for three seasons. Since 1988, he has been the head coach of The Seville national club team – a team which has won ten regional championships under his tutelage. In 1993, he founded the Seville Water Polo Foundation, an organization for which he currently serves as President.

Peter and his wife, Marisol, currently reside in Seville, Spain with their two children, Peter and Paolo.